Inspiring Interiors

from **Armstrong**™ 1950s

C. Eugene Moore

4880 Lower Valley Road, Atglen, PA 19310

Dedication

With love, this book is dedicated to my wife, Jan, who knows even more about creating the perfect home than Armstrong does.

Moore, C. Eugene, 1931-
    Inspiring interiors from Armstrong 1950s / C. Eugene Moore.
        p.   cm.
    ISBN 0-7643-0458-5 (pbk.)
    1. Interior decoration --United States--History--20th century--Themes, motives. 2. Armstrong World Industries. I. Title.
NK2004.3.A74M66   1998
747.213'09'04--dc21   97-42009
                                            CIP

Book design by Blair Loughrey

ISBN: 0-7643-0458-5
Printed in Hong Kong

Published by Schiffer Publishing Ltd.
4880 Lower Valley Road
Atglen, PA 19310
Phone: (610) 593-1777; Fax: (610) 593-2002
E-mail: Schifferbk@aol.com
Please write for a free catalog.
This book may be purchased from the publisher.
Please include $3.95 for shipping.

Please try your bookstore first.

We are interested in hearing from authors with book ideas on related subjects.

Contents

Acknowledgments

The room interiors depicted in this book all belong to Armstrong World Industries, Inc. (or, as it was known back in the 1950s, Armstrong Cork Company). They were designed, constructed, lighted, and photographed by a team of energetically talented Armstrong employees who poured their creative musings into the development of rooms that can inspire almost anyone with their beauty, their practicality, and their enduring charm.

There may never have been another company that over the years has provided more lasting attention to the home interior than Armstrong. And always, always this was done in the best of taste. I have attempted to maintain those high standards as I gathered the information for this volume; and it's important for the reader to know that if I sometimes failed to do so, the fault is mine and not Armstrong's.

This book could not have been compiled and written without the cooperation of Armstrong and its people. Especially helpful to me were Douglas E. Winters, David D. Wilson, Camilla Collova, James P. Kendig, Cynthia E. Hornberger, Susan I. Wood, and Patricia A. Kirchner, and I give them my thanks for their patience and understanding.

A special word of appreciation is due to Rose M. Fronczak, keeper of the company's archives. Not only did she open the door to the rich historical treasures within her purview, but also she lighted my way through them with valuable insights and suggestions. She herself is a treasure (though not yet a *historical* treasure!).

The greatest acknowledgment of all must go to the parade of interior designers, past and current, who have created such beautiful rooms. To many people, these rooms exemplify Armstrong as nothing else does. The designers have left a wonderful legacy for us all, and it is with immense pride that I had the pleasure of associating with many of them during my years at Armstrong.

Introduction

Think about this.

It's almost as unusual for a company to live a hundred years as for a human being. Not many companies in America manage to exist for a full century, at least not many under one common chain of management.

But here's Armstrong World Industries, Inc., born in 1860 and today going stronger than ever. For many of the years since its founding, the company has been a style leader in its field, generating interior design ideas that American families could adapt for their own home interiors.

Armstrong had its beginnings at Pittsburgh as a two-man shop for cutting cork stoppers by hand. For years it was known as Armstrong Cork Company, and certainly cork represented an important element in the early years of its existence. The manufacture of linoleum flooring began in 1909 at Lancaster, Pennsylvania, which twenty years later would become the headquarters for the company. And even linoleum had a tie to cork. For in those days this unusual raw material, finely ground, was included in the linoleum mix to provide added resilience and stability.

Linoleum in the Home

Linoleum, which had been invented in England, was considered a utilitarian product, a desirable material for the kitchen floor but inherently bland and uninteresting. Armstrong's management people, though, were perceptive enough to see other possibilities. They began speaking of linoleum as "a floor, not a floor covering." They wanted linoleum to be considered for every room in the home, not just the kitchen. They urged their wholesale distributors and retailers to "sell the idea, not the patterns."

To make their dreams come true, the product had to excite the consumer. One way to do this was with better styling of the product itself; so Armstrong expanded its line of linoleum, introducing new designs, new colors in styles never before seen in flooring. A second way was to show people how they could *decorate their homes* around the flooring, a design element that was being given new importance by the direction the company was moving.

National Advertising

On September 1, 1917, in *The Saturday Evening Post*, Armstrong ran its first national consumer advertisement for linoleum. The page cost $5,000. This was the start of one of the nation's longest-running advertising programs, a series of ads that continues today.

Soon after the first ad appeared, the company began offering its first decorating book. It had enlisted Frank Parsons, one of the nation's best-known authorities in home decoration, to prepare the book.

A decorating book was a good start. But could Armstrong also find a way to give more direct personal assistance to homeowners? Inquiries led the company to Hazel Dell Brown, at that time a supervisor of art in the Indianapolis school system. At first Mrs. Brown was unconvinced: What need did a linoleum company have for an interior decorator? Finally she relented, and soon her work with the Armstrong Bureau of Interior Decoration was being featured in the company's advertising.

New Ideas for Interior Designs

Probably no one could have fully foreseen the result. For Hazel Dell Brown and the talented inte-

rior designers who would follow her would have an enormous impact on the direction Armstrong's advertising would take. In the years to come they would generate thousands of practicable ideas that America's families could draw on. They helped to establish the company as one of America's truly important influences in the design of residential interiors.

Along the way Armstrong would introduce other products to its resilient flooring line, especially vinyl and no-wax types, and these represented improvements that would gradually diminish the importance of linoleum. By August 10, 1974, when the company discontinued linoleum production, it had produced 957 million square yards of this material. That was enough to stretch to the moon in a path six feet wide, with enough left to circle the moon four times!

In 1980 the corporation changed its name from Armstrong Cork Company to Armstrong World Industries, Inc., better to reflect the global presence it had become.

The 1950s

In Armstrong's long history, the decade of the 1950s stands out as a historical highlight for anyone interested in following residential interior design.

For the company this was a decade of unusual growth. It was responding to the demand that had been created by the enforced deprivations of World War II, which had ended in 1945. The interior designers cranked up their creativity with room interiors intended to meet a variety of consumer inter-

ests, while always presenting tasteful, down-to-earth ideas that homeowners would be proud to claim as their own.

Important changes were taking place in America's housing. World War II veterans, now with brides, were beginning their families. At first many squeezed into tiny apartments created within the homes of their parents or parents-in-law. This would not satisfy them for long. And the GI Bill, which offered the possibility of low-interest mortgage loans for the veterans, gave them an added reason to yearn for homes of their own.

Levittowns Begin

A housing developer named William J. Levitt came up with one answer. He established the country's first mass-produced suburb. In former potato fields on Long Island, forty miles east of New York City, Levitt turned the veterans' dreams into reality by building boxy, four-and-a-half-room Cape Cod-style homes on lots sixty by a hundred feet in size. The first of his houses were offered to the public in 1947. By the time he finished constructing Levittown, New York, he had covered 7.3 square miles with Cape Cods and ranch houses in slightly different variations. The returning GIs, these young men who together with their wives would produce the Baby Boom and change the world, lined up to buy the new houses.

Levitt had built an entire town. He went on to build two more, one in Pennsylvania and one in New Jersey. His houses were built without basements. Each had four rooms, a bath, and an attic that could be finished to provide more space for

an expanding family. Included were a Bendix washing machine, a GE refrigerator, a Hotpoint electric range, and steel kitchen cabinets. Later models would add a built-in television set.

Visualize yourself as moving into one of Levitt's houses. You had earned the title of homeowner, pleased to be able to nestle your family in comfortable new quarters at an affordable price. You took pride in this, and justifiably so. And yet. And yet. As you looked out your front door, you saw the house across the street, virtually identical to yours. The houses on either side of you? Virtually identical to yours.

Consciously or subconsciously, the new owners of the houses in Levittown began to exert their own personalities in the homes they lived in. If the neighbors planted an oak in their front yard, we'll plant a maple in ours. If they added green shutters, we'll add red window boxes. In particular, we'll decorate the interior of our home to establish our own individual tastes.

Similar decisions were being made in the other, if generally smaller, housing tracts springing up across the United States.

Do-It-Yourself

By the dawning of the 1950s, this had resulted in a wonderful opportunity for Armstrong. Already experienced in offering decorating ideas, the company now was in a position to help consumers improve their homes with a burgeoning assortment of products, including some types that they themselves could install. Armstrong ads took flight, with a succession of room interiors that cried out to those who wanted to make their homes more appealing and more individualistic.

Living was in many respects simpler then. The typical family had one automobile, one television set, one bathroom. One wage-earner. No videocasette recorder, no compact disc player, no entertainment center, no remote control device, no charge card, no home air conditioning, no jacuzzi or hot tub, no centralized vacuum system, no microwave oven. Certainly no home computer.

During the '50s, this began to change. Now some houses offered a bathroom off the master bedroom. Residential acoustical ceilings were introduced. The television-watching room became the recreation room, which became the family room, now an added space in the home. The demand grew for easier maintenance throughout.

Armstrong Leads the Way

Armstrong responded to such changes. And in many ways it led the parade, as it offered idea after idea to meet the growing demands Americans were placing on the homes in which they spent so much of their time.

Out of the ferment of the '50s came the rooms you'll find in this book. As you look through its pages I believe you'll be struck by how modern the rooms are, at least in the sense that they offer decorating tips and suggestions that now, several decades later, can still be adapted for your home.

I hope you will use the book in this way—and that you find the ideas it provides helpful in making your own home more attractive, more comfortable, and easier to care for.

Chapter 1

Kitchens

The rhythm of the kitchen is the heartbeat of the home. In some respects, this is the most important space within the house, and it's probably the room most visited through the daylight hours. In its advertisements of the 1950s, Armstrong spread a lot of loving attention on the kitchen, filling its ads with decorative, workable ideas that members of a family could use in their own home to make life easier and more enjoyable.

A valentine the size of a kitchen. Is the kitchen a "room for romance"? In this home, certainly! Its decor was inspired by an old-fashioned valentine card, all frothy with lace. The motif is captured in wooden cutouts that are used as dividing screens and as a valance to hide the lighting over the counter, sink, and kitchen range areas. The painted scrollwork over the doorway extends the theme. Hearts and lovebirds are sprinkled throughout, even in the mirror (see inset) and on cupboard doors. A sunny floor of linoleum provides an easy-to-wipe-up surface in the event of spills. It's in a design known as Spatter, which resembles the splatterdash effect popular in some areas during the American Colonial period. And is that a sure-enough live bird in the cage above the sink? No. This one is a realistic simulation, and it's there just to help carry out the romantic theme.

Well-planned for a working woman. When you're holding down a job in addition to being a homemaker, you appreciate the special touches that go into a kitchen like this one. It's arranged to save time and steps. If you're rushed, or just feel like letting the dishes go, you can hide everything in the food preparation area by pulling down a venetian blind. Everything's within arm's reach. A file cabinet was the inspiration for the set of drawers right next to the kitchen range; that's where the pots and pans are stored. China and glassware are held in brackets on a swingaway door near the eat-in counter at left. And the linoleum flooring is coved right up the wall, so there's no corner to catch dirt.

A corner six feet square—and what versatility! In the design of this room, Armstrong showed how a corner of the kitchen could become "the most valuable space in the house." Most of the time, the area is used as a playpen with the adjustable table flat on the floor. The family's toddler can play here, in sight of Mom while she prepares a meal nearby. At breakfast time (inset 1) the table is pulled up to normal height so meals can be served conveniently. All the tableware is kept in the cupboard behind the table, and places can be set without the waste of a step. Smooth-surface flooring covers the floor and the tabletop in this corner, to make cleaning up easier. Older children start their playtime as soon as they reach home from kindergarten (inset 2); now the table is moved halfway down, just the right height for them. Toys are kept in the low storage bins, within easy reach. When the family wishes to entertain (inset 3), the table pulls up to waist level to serve as a refreshment bar. The marbleized effect of the linoleum in the corner, six feet by six feet in size, harmonizes with the embossed inlaid linoleum in a tile design that's used in the rest of the kitchen.

1

2

3

"No bigger than a bird cage." You move into a home that's adequate for your family, but with a kitchen that is tiny. How do you deal with this? Here's one answer. The floor is the largest decorative element in the room, so start with that. A black marbleized linoleum effect, inset with white marbleized linoleum, gives the appearance of more space. For added storage, new corner cupboards and cabinets were fitted with lazy susan shelves that make it easy to get at things. Thin black bars travel up the cabinets, up the walls, and across the ceiling. They break the monotony of an all-white room and whimsically carry out the "bird cage" theme, as do the painted birds in painted cages. Because of the slide-out snack bars (see inset), it's even possible for two people to eat in this small but efficient kitchen.

Rearranged design saves a hundred steps every day. It wasn't planned, exactly. But when her refrigerator was moved temporarily to the center of her kitchen, the homemaker soon found she liked it that way. Now the refrigerator was right at hand, next to the sink and the stove. Never had she been able to cook a meal with so little effort and waste motion. She calculated that the new setup saved her about a hundred steps a day. Other benefits turned up, also. Now she found that she had room behind the refrigerator for the dining nook she had always wanted. And she could get an extra cabinet and add storage and work space in an island arrangement. She could get even more storage room with shallow cabinets on the wall space the refrigerator had been occupying.

Everything aimed at easy care. In this small but well-laid-out kitchen, all the decorative elements were chosen with maintenance in mind. For a quick spruce-up after a meal, every surface—from the smooth resilient flooring to the colorful porcelain face on the steel-base wall tiles— wipes clean with a damp cloth. The breakfast bar at right is within easy reach of the food-preparation area, though it is hidden from sight by a partial wall that doubles as a storage space.

Big idea for small-kitchen planning. Every homemaker wants lots of cabinets and plenty of counter space. Trouble is, in a small kitchen they take up too much room. Even if the kitchen is nine feet wide, ordinary two-foot cabinets down both sides of the room cut the floor space to five feet. In this kitchen the cabinets are only half the usual depth. But counter space has not been sacrificed because the countertops swing up out of the way when not in use, forming the bottom doors that close off the upper cabinets (see inset). Above the shelves, the overhead cabinets are easy to reach with a step stool that turns into a breakfast table when you lift the drop leaves. When it's in front of the settee at right, you have a place for dining; yet there's no space lost when it's not being used as a table. Notice that the cabinets are several inches off the floor to reduce stooping, with the linoleum flooring coved up underneath to eliminate dirt-catching corners.

A kitchen clipped out of the magazines. If you're one of those people who go through magazines with a pair of scissors in hand, cutting out recipes and decorating ideas to paste into your scrapbook, you'll recognize the appeal of this room. Here the bareness of the white cabinets is relieved in a colorful way by photographs of everything from soups to desserts clipped from magazine articles. It's a regular art gallery of menu ideas, ready at hand. At right is a schoolteacher desk, built right into the counter. Those ten small drawers are just the right size for filing recipe cards, and you can work at the desk either standing up or sitting down. The telephone is close at hand for ordering. And with its desk, this kitchen becomes a sunny, pleasant spot for writing letters in the afternoon.

A small kitchen exploding with ideas. This room is full of surprises. Almost every one of its decorative elements holds a practical idea that saves time, labor and maintenance. See that attractive row of little drawers under the window? They're for tea, coffee, and spices. At a glance you can see what you have. Just to their right are soaps and cleaning powders, within easy reach. The strings stretched across the window add interest to the decor— and mean no curtains to wash. The panel below the sink, with the handle on it, hides a step stool (inset 1). It rolls around easily, yet stays put when you step on it. Special spring casters do the trick. The cabinets with the cake and flowers on them are regular work counters when the tops are closed. Open them up and they make wonderful lunch bars (inset 2). Oh yes, the little red stool? It was made from a tractor seat!

1

2

Making an old room look new. A bit of redesign, coupled with furnishings chosen for easy maintenance, can transform a well-worn kitchen into one that's modern and convenient. The addition of a wall separates the stove and sink from the eat-in area, with a pass-through that can be closed off with folding doors. Utensils hang conveniently above the kitchen range. Walls and floor are covered with smooth, easy-to-clean surfaces.

Where baking is fun. Some homemakers find that turning out delicious French pastries helps to satisfy their creative instincts in a way that's greatly appreciated! Here's a kitchen planned especially for those who love to bake. At the marble-topped baking counter at right, cookbooks are nearby, just where they're needed. Most-used utensils are in a trough right above the counter. Recipe cards are clipped onto the top lid, where they're easy to read, easy to keep clean. Twin ovens help speed the baking, and the doors on all the cabinets slide so they're never in the way. Baking involves spreading flour on more than the counter, inevitably; but the resilient flooring makes spills easy to wipe up. The pastry shelves convert to a dining table (see inset), so the kitchen also doubles as a convenient place for family meals.

Ideas inspired by a soda fountain. How do some short-order cooks manage to whip up a meal so fast? Part of the answer lies in the efficient arrangement of their kitchens, with everything reachable. You can set up your own kitchen like this, too. Here working areas, including a big cutting board, are centralized at one end of the room. Open shelves of varying widths provide extra shelf space and eliminate the cost of doors. Bins for flour and sugar and such are built in along the back of the sink, in real soda fountain style. You could even have a glass case for displaying cakes and pies. Concentrating working areas at one end leaves room for a small booth for dining. Its table has a special folding feature. Before and after meals, its top offers extra counter area. During meals, part of the top folds against the wall (see inset); pictures on the outside become part of the decoration. In the linoleum flooring, transverse stripes make the narrow room look wider.

Old-fashioned charm in a modern kitchen. Remember how your grandmother would give you "a cookie for each hand"? Her kitchen was always warm and friendly, even though it wasn't up-to-date by today's standards. This room thinks back to her time. It dresses modern conveniences in a style that she'd feel comfortable with. Spatter patterns in the linoleum floor reflect the splatterdash wooden floors of Colonial America. The combination work counter-lunch bar is on wheels so it can be moved about. It has a lazy susan at the end, for utensils, and the table-top doubles as shelf space to hold work in progress—such as Grandma's cookies. The sampler above the range can be homemade to reflect individual tastes.

Family living fits into this kitchen. If you like to have your family's activities centered around the home, this kitchen should have a special interest for you. It's designed to encourage that wonderful American custom of family gathering. With the lure of a crackling fire, everyone will want to dine in the kitchen. But it's large enough to allow you to invite friends in, also. Pleasant surroundings. But you'll appreciate its practical side as well. The waist-high oven right next to the counter could hardly be more convenient. And side-by-side stoves provide much-needed additional cooking units. When you're through with the meal preparation, cover the stove with its top (see inset) and you have extra work space or a refreshment bar. Almost seamless and flashed up the wall, the linoleum flooring offers few places for dirt to hide.

Easy to care for. Look at the work-saving features in this kitchen, and you'll find that each of them also adds to the appeal of the room. The natural wood finish on the cabinets adds warmth to the decorative scheme, and it doesn't show dirt readily. The table top and work counters are covered with a colorful linoleum sheet material, and they swish clean with a damp cloth. For storage efficiency, cupboard space extends right to the ceiling. The stepladder slides along a rail that also serves as a rack for dishtowels. At right a shelf provides extra work space but folds out of sight when not in use. The flooring is a linoleum-like tile, installed in a custom design effect.

Here you'll find what you're looking for. Next time you're scrambling through the cupboard drawers looking for a cookie cutter or searching in vain to find a piece of string to tie up a roast, remember this kitchen. It's for people who want a place for everything. Cupboards? More than sixty of them in this one room. Each is intended to hold specific items. You automatically put everything back where it belongs. And next time you want something, it's there. Vegetables are stored under the sink. Pots and pans are where they should be, right under the stove. Cook a roast and it goes from oven to chopping block, where it can be carved immediately and placed on the serve-through counter with no waste motion. The top cupboards over the sink can be opened from the dining room side, too, and that's a big help when setting the table. This kitchen is planned around individual tasks, and there's even one corner devoted to baking (see inset).

1

2

Conversion of an older home. During the 1950s Armstrong took over a country house near Lancaster, Pennsylvania, years old but structurally sound. It reworked every room to show what miracles could be performed with new ideas to make the home more inviting, more livable. The kitchen exemplifies the result of this project. Besides being decorative, each of the big squares on the wall opens for storage space. The dining table on wheels can be rolled about for added counter space wherever

and whenever it's needed. Two apartment-sized ranges, side by side, provide double oven space and cost less than one large range. Almost everything in the old kitchen (inset 1) was outdated, including its linoleum floor. Although the old flooring was still serviceable after twenty years of use, it was replaced by a new design in an embossed effect. Unlike the old kitchen, the renovated model has lots of storage space (inset 2).

Looks as though this house has a maid—but it doesn't. A large kitchen can be a blessing. But when it's in an older house, sometimes you feel that you must begin preparing lunch before you've had time to clear away the breakfast dishes. Here's how one homemaker was able to quit being a slave to the clock. The secret was in remodeling the kitchen and in using easy-maintenance materials. Adding a partition made a compact and more efficient work center and gained space for a laundry. Having an eating bar on the other side of the partition helped, especially with that serve-through right behind the stove. The colors in the new linoleum flooring helped separate the two areas of the room visually. Because the scroll inset cut from one color of linoleum was interchanged with the other, there was no wasted material in this two-color design.

For a lady who loves to cook. Some people really enjoy cooking, and they're good at it. Such people deserve a kitchen like this. It's filled with fingertip conveniences intended to make every hour spent in it pleasant and productive. Look at that herb hothouse. Built right out from the kitchen window, it permits you to pluck fresh herbs at any season. The "mobile" light fixture also serves as a rack for utensils. It's counterbalanced, so frequently used utensils are within easy reach yet can be pushed up and out of the way when not needed. Sharp knives are in a separate rack at the end of the counter, out of reach of the younger children. The work table, topped with a generous-sized butcher block, slides along the floor to wherever you want it. Cleaning up afterward, usually the most tiresome of cooking chores, is no problem. Lettuce leaves and other food trimmings disappear down a hole in the counter into an enamel pan for easy disposal. Friends can sit in the student chairs and enjoy the products of this "cooking kitchen" while they admire its built-in beauty and convenience.

Bringing the outdoors inside. Some people wish they could enjoy outdoor living all through the year. This kitchen takes them a long way toward that goal. The glass window wall brings the color of the terrace garden right into the room. The oven and stove are placed so that you can get an out-of-doors feeling even while you're cooking. And the view from the snack bar lets you enjoy the pleasures of outdoor eating even when chilly weather keeps you inside. During warmer seasons, it's convenient to cook indoors, eat outdoors because the sink, stove, and oven lead in assembly-line order to the terrace. The terrace lends this kitchen its color scheme, too. For example, note the whitewashed wall behind the sink counter. It's made of rough brick like the flower-banked fireplace outside. Even the rubber tile floor has an air of outdoors, as its white and lush brown colorings echo the natural beauty of the flagstones on the terrace.

Decorative unity in an open-plan interior. Open planning, using as few interior walls as possible, can make a small house appear to be larger than it is. But it also can present a problem, because it creates the need for decorative unity between living areas. Here a floor of embossed linoleum in a flagstone design achieves this in an attractive manner. The colors chosen for the room are taken from the accent colors of the flooring material. Other features add grace and convenience to the open planning. For example, the island counter separating the kitchen from the dining area has a pass-through for simpler serving. The table includes drawers with ready-at-hand items used at mealtime. A bank of suspended lights illuminates the color of the potted plants in the garden window.

A Continental look right at home. This room was inspired when a homemaker was leafing through her daughter's geography textbook, looking at color pictures of the beautiful items made in Europe. What really caught her eye were blue Meissen china from Germany and delft blue tiles made in the Netherlands. When she turned the page and came across French Provincial furniture, she was committed to a redo of her kitchen. It helped when she found that she could install rubber tile in colors to match the accessories she had in mind. The remodeling job turned out to be less expensive than she had thought. Her husband, good with tools, was drafted to build the cabinets. And the molding effect, though it looks like costly carving, is merely painted onto the face of the cabinets. Now this family can dine in Continental splendor every night.

Integrating the kitchen fully into family living. A small, cramped kitchen, isolated by walls from the rest of the house, can be turned into a centerpiece for the family, with a bit of creative thought given to its proper place in the home. Here the kitchen stayed just where it was. But look how open and inviting it is now. An attached garage provided space for a beautiful, modern family activities room. The new floor was built up from the garage level, then finished with linoleum in a distinctive design that extends into the kitchen to unite both areas decoratively. Nobody would recognize the old garage now, as it has become a family recreation room with a dining area to supplement the home's more formal dining room. A lavatory has been added behind the couch at right. Spacious windows bring in lots of light.

What does the word "modern" mean to you? To most interior decorators, it represents a blend of whatever elements make a home more attractive and easier to live in. This kitchen contains a number of such elements, combined in an appealing unity. A large garden window floods the space with light, allowing the potted flowers to become part of the decorative scheme. The hanging ham and onions make it plain that this place is about food. Their rusticity is balanced by the sparkling glassware arranged in formal rows on the shelves. A screen hides the food preparation area from the dining room at left. Linoleum installed in transverse stripes gives the illusion of added width, increasing the room's feeling of openness.

Go ahead and get gleeful. If you like to sing while you work, this kitchen would sing along with you. It has a lighthearted look, but don't let that mislead you. Its purpose is quite serious in aiming to reduce the chores of preparing and serving food. The counter, reachable from all sides, extends into the room from the stove out almost to the breakfast bar. Utensils, pots and pans, and serving dishes are kept in this counter and in the drawers next to the refrigerator. Plates and silverware are in the cupboards in the eat-in part of the room. When the sun beams too warmly through the window wall, a roll-down screen helps to cool everything to a more comfortable level. And the wallpaper applied to the sides of the counter means that, as you work and eat in this kitchen, butterflies are flitting playfully near you.

Children welcome underfoot. The homemaker with young children can keep an eye on them while she spends her time in this well-designed kitchen-dining area. The dining table is just a step away from the sink, yet separated from it so that there's a minimum of "kitcheny" atmosphere. The whole area is compact, but look how much storage space it incorporates. Mom can readily reach the items she needs, but they're up and out of the grasp of toddlers. The children can play on the floor without damaging its vinyl-content surface. This surface isn't harmed by grease and splatter, either, and crumbs sweep away in an instant. The flooring tile is installed in a layout that sets apart the dining area from the kitchen without sacrificing decorative unity.

You can live all over this home. In an up-to-date house with open planning, you can enjoy a fuller, freer life. There are no barriers to insist that you eat in one place, relax here, or entertain there. You choose the activity, and you decide where you'll do what you wish to do. Even the outdoors can become a part of your home, when the interior is decoratively related to the textures and colors one finds outside. Here the warmth of natural wood grains and multicolored bricks reflects the atmosphere of the patio garden just beyond the window walls. Even the flooring, of embossed inlaid linoleum in a brick effect, helps to carry out the openness of the home design. An exposed-beam ceiling conveys the feeling of comfortable country living.

A kitchen can be a work of art. In today's kitchens, beauty and efficiency are linked. Here's one that proves it. The appliances and storage units are framed together in a striking wall composition, reminiscent of the geometric painting done by European masters. And the linoleum flooring, with its inset stripes in a contrasting color, carries out the visual theme. At first glance the room appears almost carelessly spacious and open. But take a second look, and you begin to appreciate how much efficiency is built into its design. Ample storage cupboards and drawers, a built-in desk, and a stove in the peninsular counter with its vent hood above are some of its features. Don't you know that at every mealtime her family appreciates the "works of art" that the homemaker produces in this setting?

Wrap it around the dining room. Here's a useful idea for remodeling a big old kitchen. Or for including in a new house. In this instance, the kitchen in an older home was divided by an L-shaped partition. Outside the L is the new step-saving kitchen. Wrapped inside (see inset) is a modern dining area. Close the shutters and you have two separate rooms. Open them and both rooms are joined into one. The flooring of a vinyl sheet material carries the color scheme right through, with accents sprinkled through the basic blue, white and gray effect. At the outside corner of the L, a cupboard door swings open to reveal pots and pans, close by the stove. And the pass-through counters make it as easy to clear away the dining room after a meal as it was to serve the food earlier.

Where it's always "good morning."
When you're greeted by a cheerful kitchen like this, getting up and making breakfast is almost fun. It's bright and radiant even on gray, chilly mornings because its warmth is built in. The reds and yellows that give it life are chosen from the flooring of linoleum and repeated all around the room in its other decorative elements. The lines of the cupboards are sheer and straight, promising easy maintenance. Of course the window wall helps, too. It invites the sun to come in, splashing its light everywhere and helping to open up an already appealing room layout. Birds gather in the terrace garden just outside, adding their songs to the cheery setting. Who could be downhearted in such a room?

An old-fashioned look in a new-fashioned home. Can you remember the days when lots of houses had kitchen floors made of bricks? Old-fashioned, maybe, but nice. How permanent, how friendly the bricks looked, gleaming after their morning scrubdown. (Scrubdown? Ah, there was the rub!) Here's the modern counterpart for the new-fashioned home. It's resilient flooring in a brick design. It has all the charm of true brick, right down to the embossed grout lines, but it doesn't constantly call out for hard scrubbing. Relatively infrequent maintenance is enough to keep the floor bright and beautiful. And you can see right away how well it goes with the other features of this modern home. The eat-in portion of the kitchen is for quick family meals, while the more formal dining room is close at hand. And the rolling tea cart at right can be used in either area.

An air of distinction. The woman who planned this kitchen didn't miss a lot. She knew she was going to spend much of each day here, and she decided from the beginning that her new kitchen was going to be just right for her. She wanted it to be light and airy. So she situated the countertops and other important work areas right inside sumptuous stretches of glass, and now the sunlight keeps her company all day. The room is informal, and that's what she preferred. But she wanted it to have a look of elegance, too. When guests come into this kitchen—and they almost all want to—they remember the striking black-and-white design of the flooring and the life and elegance it lends to the room. Even the cupboards have a light, open appearance. They give a tantalizing glimpse at the objects they contain through mesh screens on their doors.

Go ahead and mix colors. The colored appliances available today can cause a decorating dilemma. Let's say you want this brand of oven, that brand of dishwasher. Will they match? Probably not. Or maybe you collect your colored appliances one by one over a period of years. What happens to your color scheme in the meanwhile? As this kitchen shows, it is possible to mix colors freely and still have an attractive result. Here's the secret: let your appliances set the color scheme. With paint and imagination, you can assure that the other decorating elements in the room harmonize with the various colors of the appliances. Be sure to choose a flooring material that brings everything together. This kitchen has a terrazzo-like vinyl flooring in a pattern that goes with all the major colors in the room.

Should a kitchen be just a place to cook? In many a home, the kitchen somehow is the magnet that pulls the family together. Here's one that says, "Yes, that's just what we want," then goes to work to make it happen. It's a place where toddlers can play safely and the other children can come to tell all about their adventures at school. Here Mom and Dad can relax in the evening and discuss the ups and downs of the day. Count the activities it can comfortably accommodate. Cooking, dining and meal clean-up. Playing with toys and games. Quiet reading. Television watching. *Bird* watching through the large window wall. And on a chilly winter evening, the family can gather at the fireplace for popcorn and hot chocolate. It's a step-saver, too. The room is spacious and open, yet none of its activities is more than a few paces away.

Nature comes indoors. Some interior designers have found that the textures and colors of the outdoors adapt themselves well to the interiors of today's houses. Something warm and friendly can occur when this natural look is effectively achieved. Wood, brick, and even the appearance of worn, rounded pebbles are brought together in this kitchen, with no sacrifice of modern convenience and efficiency. The surface of the flooring is gently embossed between the "pebbles" for a more realistic design effect. Potatoes and other staples are stored in a lazy susan close by the sink. Items used in meal preparation form attractive wall hangings. For example, the breadboard is within easy reach, and it also can be used to serve hors d'oeuvres when guests arrive.

Did somebody say "festive"?
If you'd like a kitchen that'll put you in the mood for lighthearted levity, take a look. This one's fitted out for fun. Decorating such a room can be an easy job for any homemaker, experienced or not. It helps to follow a few rules. First, start with the floor; it's the largest unit you have to work with in the entire scheme. Second, don't forget that you may want to change colors later on, so choose a floor that will go with several color schemes—like this polka dot design in linoleum. Third, pick up at least one of the floor's colors and use it lavishly around the room. Check out the added touches that make this room work. Wrought iron screens, which help to separate the kitchen from the breakfast area, echo the design of the wicker chair backs. A striped "circus" awning just outside the window becomes part of the interior design. And a porcelain cat on the countertop smiles her approval of the whole effect.

The "right-at-your-fingertips" kitchen. To many a homemaker, no kitchen is ever quite large enough to hold everything that's needed. One would think that counters jutting out into the limited space would create cramped conditions. But look again. Here the counters are strategically placed for efficient organization of work. Sink, refrigerator, oven, range, all are just a pace or two away from the others. At the sink counter, you can sit in comfort while preparing the evening's salad. Lighting fixtures set into the ceiling are out of the way while giving plenty of illumination where it's most important. The stripes in the vinyl flooring are more than just decorative. They also conceal the seams in the flooring; and since it comes in a sheet form, only two seams are needed in this entire kitchen. Now. Would someone please pick up that phone?

A touch of the East. You've traveled to faraway places, or at least you've read about them. And you'd really like to express yourself by decorating a portion of your home in an unforgettable, exotic fashion. Well, why not, especially when it's so easy to do? This home has an Oriental flavor, and it doesn't give up anything in comfort and beauty. The bamboo-like special insets in the vinyl flooring set the pace. They're reflective of the chairs around the dining table (and of the actual bamboo growing just outside the window). The special furnishings, such as the lacquered chest, the tall rice-paper lamp, the garden lantern, and the Japanese doll, look as if they must have cost a lot during a trip to the Far East. Actually, every one of them was obtainable locally; and they inexpensively add just the right touch to the interior theme of this home.

Chapter 2

Dining rooms

In a typical American home, the dining room is one of the two most guest-oriented areas—the other being the living room. Some dining rooms are formal, and Armstrong shows how these can be elegant without being stuffy. Others are as warm and friendly as a neighbor's wave. Here we find examples of both. The rooms in this section are full of stylish decorating ideas that you'll enjoy searching out. Which ones could be adapted to your own home?

When you run out of money, roll up your sleeves. The young couple who own this home built it on a shoestring. Before they were through, they found that the shoestring wasn't long enough. The furniture came last, so that's where they had to cut. But wait a minute. Where did all those authentic-looking Oriental pieces come from? The couple put their ingenuity to work. The Chinese peel chairs were unfinished and quite inexpensive. While the wife applied the varnish to those, her husband built the bamboo table. Yes, built it himself. They laughed at him, he says, when he went down to the hardware store and bought their entire supply of fishing poles. But nobody laughs at what he did with them. And nobody guesses that there are two old crates under the bamboo and that the top is just a sheet of plywood, covered with plain linoleum. Speaking of linoleum, the special inset in the flooring helps this dining room carry through its striking Chinese Modern look.

Built on a concrete slab, a house needs a special floor. Ordinary floors won't do for a basementless house built directly on a concrete slab in contact with the ground. The problem is that moisture from the earth rises through the concrete, picking up alkali as it moves to the surface. When flooring is put over the concrete, the alkaline moisture has nowhere to go. It loses its ability to evaporate. And this can cause some types of flooring to deteriorate. But there are ways of dealing with this problem. One answer is shown in this house. Its asphalt tile flooring was developed especially to withstand the alkaline moisture in concrete floor slabs of basements and basementless houses. Contrasting bands of tile and feature strips extend from the dining room into the living room to provide a unified look in this warm and friendly home.

See what a difference color makes. The use of well-chosen color can mean a dramatic transformation in almost any room. Many people tend to be too conservative when they decorate. They want rich color, and they like its effect. But when it comes right down to using it, they lose their nerve. That's why we see so many dull, no-personality rooms (see above). The picture shows what a splash of color can do. It proves how easy it is to change the entire character of a room, with no major structural alterations—just with color. Every room, modern or traditional, needs color; and the materials available today make it easy to expand the possibilities. As an example, in the redecorated room see how much more attractive the flooring is, with its contrasting border, than the drab flooring in the "before" picture.

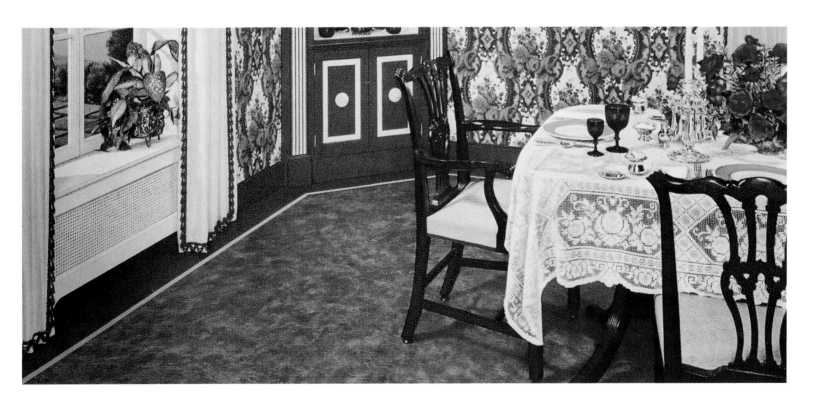

When a room is outdated. The bold use of color and accessories can restore interest in a room that over the years has gradually sunk into boredom. There was nothing wrong with the furnishings in this dining room (see inset). The room was practical and livable, but it suffered from one major fault: outmoded decoration. Its appearance dated back to the time when people were afraid to use color. The nicely styled furniture deserved something better than this. But now look! Something important takes place when the color shackles are thrown off. Because of their large areas, walls and floors are the most logical places to add the color accents you want every room to have. Here the walls are emblazoned with the designs of a strong wallpaper pattern. The linoleum flooring is dressed up with a beautifully rendered scroll effect. And a sculptured eagle wall hanging gives its blessing to the now-interesting overall effect.

Dining room, living room, party room—without crowding. Here's a room designed to solve the problems of costly space and still provide for the activities of a modern family. The key to its versatility is the storage wall at left, with tables that combine for dining, pull apart for cards. As a dining room, the space provides a comfortable, pleasant atmosphere. When it's a living room, the tables can be pushed through the wall opening into the kitchen. Or, as you see them here (inset 1), they can be left partly out of the wall to serve as a buffet or library table. The folding chairs are stored in the wall compartments along with the table linens and dinnerware. When it's a party room (inset 2), tables and chairs are set up for two bridge foursomes. The hanging light pulls up or down for each of the room's varied functions; and the wall-to-wall linoleum flooring, partially covered with carpet, also serves every purpose of the room while holding the space together decoratively.

1

2

Can this really be the same room? Yes, but wearing two different dresses for two contrasting effects. First, the room is set for an informal buffet supper. Slipcovers are Turkish toweling trimmed with red rickrack. The floral centerpiece is in a window box planter that takes the place of the center leaf of the table. The dashing red floor, with a plain gray border, adds to the festive atmosphere. But with a few simple changes, the room puts on its formal dress (see bottom photo). Now a rug partially covers the resilient flooring. The slipcovers are removed to reveal the elegant upholstery beneath. The rakish swags at the windows have been replaced with more dignified curtains. In both of the room's personalities, an unusual lighting effect is obtained from the inexpensive tin lanterns attached to the ceiling.

Traditional furnishings in a modern home interior. In this house everything seems to go together naturally, even though the home construction is definitely contemporary and the furnishings are from an earlier period. Modern is not any one style but rather a way of living that's pleasant, comfortable, and free from unnecessary housekeeping. Let's say that you have a treasured family heirloom like the carved buffet cabinet at left. Note how it's been placed so it's the focal point of the room. Some of the furnishings dramatically catch sunlight from the window wall and skylight. A rough brick wall brings the look of the out-of-doors right inside. So does the profusion of plantings. The wall-to-wall linoleum flooring makes cleanup easy, while an area rug adds an interesting new texture to the interior.

Cut a corner, gain a dining room. Has it ever occurred to you that you can make a whole new room in your home if you already have two walls that form an L? The way to do it is to cut across the corner by constructing a new wall. And now you have a wonderful triangular room that's indoors and outdoors at the same time. If it joins the kitchen, as it does here, it makes an exciting place to dine. The floor is of alternating patterns in rubber tile. The full-sized windows in the new wall are of insulating glass and the space is heated, so this becomes a room you can use all through the year. If you roll down the curtains in the summer, you'll want to leave them up a bit so you can see the flowers blooming just outside.

New outlook for an old dining room. Elegant rooms sometimes come about through unorthodox routes. In this older house, the owners were disturbed by an unsightly view out of the window of the dining room. What should they do? Put up a high fence to block the view? Seal off the window entirely? Then an idea struck them: Instead of doing the obvious, let's open up the window and create our own view right outside. One good thought led to another, and soon they had a big window that frames a classical fountain garden. They like it so much that they arranged their dining tables so they and their guests can enjoy the view all through the meal. And the plash of falling water provides the dinnertime music.

Rain will never spoil a backyard picnic here. Did you ever plan a picnic, then have to run for cover just as you're ready to serve your guests? Rain couldn't ruin your fun if you had an all-weather, all-year-round barbecue spot like this. You might even be able to build it yourself, especially if your home has a breezeway. The furnishings are not luxurious, but they're well-suited for this type of room. Folding director-type chairs surround a redwood picnic table. A spray of flowers, waves of sunlight washing across everything (when it's not raining, that is), and a picnic free of ants and mosquitoes. It's indoor comfort for outdoor dining.

Upstairs, downstairs, even below ground level. A mountainside home with a great view calls for something special and elegant to reflect its setting. One answer is a multi-level house that carries its decorative scheme right through every room. The arrangement of lighting fixtures and ferns, along with the contrasting feature strips in the vinyl tile flooring, helps move your eye from the dining room upstairs through the ground-level foyer to the sunken living area. The massive stone wall suggests the character of the outside terrain, and all the furnishings are chosen for comfort as well as beauty. Even the exposed beams in the ceiling seem to point to nature's splendor outside the full-length windows.

When you're ruled by the budget. It happens to just about every family at times, especially when the children are in their formative years. You feel the need for a decorative upgrade in your home, yet you feel the vise tightening every time you look at the bank balance. One answer is to shrug and say, "Well, we can postpone doing anything that isn't an emergency. We'll just have to live with everything as it is." But another approach is to do what you can for now, making one small improvement at a time while not letting go of the purse-strings. In this simply furnished dining room, a new look and new comfort have been achieved just with the addition of an inexpensive fiber rug.

Can a basementless house look this sumptuous?
Yes, and yes again. The dining room and adjacent living room carry out an Oriental theme through the use of design elements treated in an unusual way. A Japanese screen is mounted tight against the wall so we can appreciate its full grandeur. It's an open-plan house; but entryways are suggested by the vertical posts, flanked in the foreground by knotted fancywork from the Far East. Note how the mesh screen is suspended near the ceiling. Shallow trays filled with pebbles and overflowing with daisy chrysanthemums serve as a counterpoint to the tall bamboo on the opposite side of the room. A few lacquered bowls and appropriate figurines complete the ensemble.

Baronial splendor in a contemporary home. The decorative elements of this house were chosen to lend it a sixteenth century appeal. The natural wood grains nicely frame the arched windows. An open-work screen at left is emblazoned with trays suggestive of the period. The unusual pierced-metal chandelier could have come right out of a European castle. The figurine and even the tankards help carry out the theme. But there is an especially modern touch in this home. Look upward. Between the beams is the sweep of an acoustical ceiling that soaks up all kinds of irritating noise. It softens the racket of children, the whirring of appliances, and the jangling of bells into gentler sounds that make a house more livable and entertaining more pleasant. This type of ceiling can be installed by do-it-yourselfers. The flooring is of linoleum in a flagstone effect (see inset).

Brought over from France? No, but the ideas behind this redecorated dining room-kitchen were. With the French Provincial furniture and the wallpaper "windows" offering a view over Paris, you might think you're in eighteenth century France. Glassware sparkles within a shallow dividing wall. That wall separates the two rooms. Another decorative element ties everything together, though. That's the embossed linoleum flooring. Its warm red-browns and hexagonal tile motif suggest a friendly old French farm kitchen. One important difference: instead of three thousand separate tiles with over a thousand feet of dirt-catching joints, the whole expanse of this linoleum has only one seam. Fitted by a craftsman, this single, almost invisible seam is so well joined that not a speck of dust hides in it.

Why would you want to leave this room? For that matter, why would you need to? So many of the family's activities are centered here. The family that remodeled it wanted their living country-style, with friendly comfort taking precedence over everything else. Because it's close to both food-preparation and dining areas, the old seed chest at left can be used to hold recipe cards, table linens, and other small items of servingware. The rustic chest near the fireplace, which fits into the room perfectly, is typical of items that can be picked up at country auctions. The high windows are positioned to invite in the afternoon sunlight. And the family even found room for laundry appliances. A floor of linoleum in a white brick design lends authenticity to the farmlike feel of the space.

For those who like wood and plenty of it. The natural grain of wood is hard to top when you're looking to achieve a warm, welcoming atmosphere in the home. The pedestal table, with its thick top, is fine for guests and most family dinners. For less formal occasions and gather-'round-the-fireside snacks, the arms of the schoolmarm chairs serve just as well. The pierced-tin chandelier echoes the look of the antique wrought iron utensils hanging at the hearth. A braided rug adds color to the wooden floor. Did we say wooden floor? Not quite. It's actually linoleum. It has all the good looks of an old pegged plank floor, but it's more practical and moderately priced. Made in six-foot widths, this flooring has few seams; and they were so expertly joined when the linoleum was put down that they're almost invisible.

Squares and circles. Elegance in room decoration can be achieved through understatement. In this dining room, the design is simplicity itself. Most of the lines are straight. The sheer rectangular feel of the table and chairs, the cross-hatched effect of the entryway screen, even the shape of the unusual fanlight above the door. But for contrast the room offers curves, also. We find them in the wall treatment at right and in the graceful sweep of the banisters. Now take a close look at the flooring. It features a subtle surface comprising thousands of small chips, like the tesserae found in old Roman courtyards. It's a rich three-dimensional effect, for you actually look down into this floor. And its tiny squares of vinyl help establish the decorative theme in the same way the straight lines do.

Living rooms

During the middle years of the twentieth century, many Americans began adding "recreation rooms" to their homes. New houses now often included what were being called "family rooms." The primary role of the living room gradually changed from a place for family "living" to a room for entertaining guests. But as this chapter shows, it was possible for the living room to take on that new responsibility while remaining an attractive, welcoming area for members of the household.

The basementless house. In the post-World War II rush to build affordable housing for growing families, many homes were erected on concrete slabs in direct contact with the ground. Such a slab can act like a wick, drawing water from the ground up through the concrete and picking up alkaline salts from the concrete as it rises to the surface. Over time, certain types of resilient flooring could be deteriorated by alkaline moisture. But this was not the case with asphalt tile, which offered the homowner durable service even under conditions of high alkalinity (though asphalt tile had limitations in some other respects). In featuring this room, Armstrong pointed out that asphalt tile also was low in cost, which fit in with the economy of building a house without a basement. Here the marbleized asphalt tile extends into the kitchen at right to provide a unified decorative appeal for the home. When entertaining guests, the family can use a foldaway door to separate the food-preparation area from the living area of the home.

A house that says "Howdy!" This home, with its wide-open appeal, seems to have been designed to make guests welcome. From the living room furniture grouped around the focal point of a fireplace, your eye travels to the dining room and its pass-through to the kitchen just beyond. And waiting just outside is the comfortable patio for sunny summer days. In winter, the home is warmed by radiant heating elements within the concrete slab it's built on. A basementless house needs a special floor, one that will resist damage from the alkalinity that works its way up through the concrete. Here the flooring is asphalt tile, a durable material that well withstands the effects of alkaline moisture. Using the same marbleized pattern throughout the home helps unify its decorative scheme.

Mixing furniture styles graciously. It really is possible to combine furnishings from various periods to achieve a harmonious effect. Treasured family hand-me-downs, newly purchased pieces, even antiques can work together if they're coordinated with care. In this room the glass flower bell at left and the marble-topped table at right both date from 1845. A couch made in 1937 (and since reupholstered) faces two Victorian chairs from 1860. The piano dates from 1910, the desk chair and upholstered chair at right from 1937, and the desk from 1939. Purchased in 1950 were the step table and the lamp it holds, the ornamental eagle over the fireplace, and the end table at right. A floor of linoleum in a grained jaspé effect and an area rug bind the room together in a unified whole.

Opposite:
Seeking ways to build at lower cost. In this home, using walls and ceilings of a wood fiber material helped reduce construction costs significantly. Yet not a bit of interior styling was sacrificed. For enhanced visual interest, the wall panels are installed in ashlar fashion over the fireplace. The same heavy fabric is incorporated in both upholstery and draperies. Figurines suggest an early Western Hemisphere influence. The hearth, with its supply of extra firewood right at hand, becomes the focal point of the room, especially because of the conversational grouping of furniture and the placement of the area rug.

Change from summer to winter in an hour. Here's an exciting idea in home decoration: two rooms in one. The change-over trick is done with four big folding screens that have a summer color scheme on one side, a winter scheme on the other. Two screens, in a refreshing summery blue and white, stand together behind the long table. Move them out, and we find that the wall they've been hiding carries the same wintertime color scheme that's on the back side of the screens. Turn the screens around, move them to the end walls so they cover the areas that have been papered in the summertime scene, and the whole room is suddenly transformed (see inset). The change from summer to winter was completed by a quick shift of curtains and by putting down an Oriental rug over the linoleum floor.

A small living room can look twice its size.
What appears to be a large living room in this home is really part dining alcove. Anyone seeing the room for the first time is impressed by its spaciousness without suspecting its double usefulness. The neat disguise is a result of furnishing the alcove to blend in with the living room. At mealtime the adjustable coffee table is raised by turning the cross legs to their high position. Draw the curtain, and you have the perfect setting for dining (see inset). As soon as the meal is over, the dining alcove disappears and again becomes part of the living room. The area gets an added look of roominess from the brick wall that serves as both outside and inside partition. Ivy, inside and out, makes the garden a part of the room. One smooth course of linoleum in both living room and dining alcove ties together the whole decorating scheme.

Quality combines with comfort. One look at this living room and you can see that its styling is far from commonplace. An appreciation of comfortable living is evident in all its furnishings, and all reflect a search for enduring quality. A well-lighted reading area is at the left, with a bookshelf within reach. Furniture in a conversation grouping, centered around the fireplace, includes a free-form coffee table. A dining wing off this room features simple but tasteful table and chairs. Flowers and living plants are placed so as to interrupt the interior with touches of nature. And the rubber tile flooring includes feature strips of a contrasting color to add dimension and visual interest. The vertical surfaces around the fireplace gain their textured beauty from sheets of natural cork.

A thrifty floor for a basementless house. Destructive alkaline moisture, always present to some degree in concrete slabs directly on the ground, would ruin some types of flooring. But asphalt tile was designed especially to resist the harmful effects of alkaline moisture; and in this basementless home, it adds a quiet beauty underfoot. The furnishings are eclectic, like those of many households. Above the fireplace, the rooster is reminiscent of folk art weathervanes. Just below, four small prints are grouped where they won't be missed. The cuckoo clock was brought home from a vacation trip. Comfortable seating around the hearth makes it a suitable area for sewing or reading. A screen at the oversized window foids open when privacy is desired.

Turning andirons into lamps. Armstrong's Idea House in Lancaster, Pennsylvania, marked the transformation of an old structure into a desirable, modern showplace through the use of exciting yet inexpensive ideas. Those tall table lamps that look so up-to-date, for example, were made by wiring a pair of old-fashioned andirons. The equally antiquated corner fireplace in the old living room (inset 1) was given a crisp new look by removing the mantelpiece and refacing with white paneling from floor to ceiling. The corner cabinet you see at the top of the other "after" photograph (inset 2) provided a novel solution to the problem of where to put the radio, phonograph, and television set. It also balanced the diagonal fireplace and gave the room a harmony and unity it had lacked before. The fireplace and corner cabinet were tied right into the whole room scheme by laying the linoleum flooring diagonally; and the yellow highlights in the floor inspired the color for the wallpaper and drapes.

1

2

An idea for living room privacy. If your front door opens directly into the living room, the room becomes a traffic lane and a target for all the dirt that's tracked in from out-of-doors. Then, too, every time someone comes to the door, he's invading the privacy of your family. If this is your situation, you may often have wished for an entrance hall. Don't rule out the possibility, for it may be easier to achieve than you think. In this home, it took little more than the introduction of a partition. It gives privacy and also serves as a built-in desk on the living room side. Make the partition deep enough for clothes hangers, and you gain a closet (see inset). The red closet interior and front door take their color cue from the flooring, an exceptionally durable tile. This flooring is installed in a layout that clearly delineates the entryway from the living room proper. Just inside the door, a Moravian star lighting fixture welcomes visitors.

The natural look in open planning. Employed couples can encounter lots of pressure and intensity. They like to think of home as a place in which they can relax in an environment that's quite different from their workplaces. That's why houses like this are built. It looks restful, with its open planning and its extensive use of natural wood. More than that, it *is* restful because it's designed for easy access and simple maintenance. The smooth linoleum flooring swishes clean with a damp mop. This flooring is installed in sheets six feet wide, so there are few seams anywhere. The trail of accent dots, specially cut and set into the flooring, shows the way to the kitchen, where they're reflected in dots of a contrasting color. And because the lighter and darker dots are the same size, they're interchangeable. That means no wasted material.

Modern ideas wake up an old house. The house was typical of those built in the 1920s—small and inconvenient, though still sound in joist and timber. Remodeling, outside and in, brought it up to date. Now it offers the advantages of modern home design. With the removal of the old partition walls, the floor plan was opened up to provide roominess. The stairway takes on a more interesting appearance with its ceiling-to-floor banisters. Their verticality is reflected in the roll-down curtain that separates the living room from the kitchen in the right background. Pull-down fixtures spread plenty of light for reading and sewing but push up out of the way when not needed. Linoleum that resembles wood graining tips its hat to the past while offering the benefits of today's easy maintenance.

Did you say "one-room house"?
Well, yes. It's a vacation home, you see. And it combines the desirable features of a full-size house in an economical, practical one-room plan. The living room sofas convert to extra beds to accommodate guests. The dining table, with its comfortable chairs, is used for games and other leisure-time activities as well as for meals. The kitchen is compact but well-equipped. A window facing the lake provides a great vista, and its opaque curtains keep out excess light when they're drawn. Best of all, when the picnic lunch is in the basket and the kids are ready to go out, you don't have to stay behind to clean up. Everything is chosen for easy care. That includes the flooring of vinyl-content tile. It's installed in contrasting patterns to visually separate the areas of the room.

Luminous luxury in split-level living. Here's a home for someone who likes restrained elegance. Nothing flashy about it. Yet see how comfortable it looks, how tasteful, how livable in all respects. One secret to this is in the lighting— everything from the high-intensity standing lamp and the more traditional table lamp in the living room to the lambency of the candlelight in the dining area. Such variety in lighting offers great flexibility in the way the home interior is presented. The soft, delicate colorings of the walls and furnishings can take on a new character with each adaptation of the lighting. And the vinyl tile that extends through this split-level area provides a quiet underfoot framework for the whole scheme.

Can you retain a traditional feeling in an open-plan home? Absolutely, if the renovation is done right. Take this older house. Its interior was outmoded, tired-looking—well, *stale* is what it was. The start of the redo was the removal of a single partition that stood between the living room and the dining area. Once that was gone, the room opened up, and so did lots of decorating possibilities. All the furnishings were chosen for comfort and enduring livability. That meant a mixing of furniture styles, but there's nothing wrong with that. It also meant that there's now room for extensive storage space along the fireplace wall. Spatter linoleum covers the floor, to assure easy care throughout the home. And the roof beams are exposed outside, adding an unusual visual effect to the view through the window.

Exposed beams and answered dreams. What is it that makes modern houses so different, so appealing? This home represents the fulfillment of a dream long held by a couple who have known for years that they wanted an open, spacious living room. Now they can afford it, and here's the result. It's a room whose inviting warmth will likely never grow pale. The fireplace is the hospitality center, as it often is, and an eye-catching painting keeps attention focused in that direction. Linoleum flooring carries out the theme in this space and into the adjacent dining room. The nubbly texture of an area rug, again, points your way to the fireplace. The treatment of the exposed-beam ceiling is unusual, but it seems a natural adjunct to the scope of the home. Potted philodendrons add height to a basically horizontal design theme.

Step inside, and you feel right at home. There's a lot about this house that makes it inviting. The room design, the furnishings, the comfort it clearly conveys. But let's concentrate on just one important element: the color. Let your eye slowly wash over the color scheme, and you'll understand how the richness of its lush hues has helped to make the home what it is. Successful use of color often starts with the floor because today's floor coverings offer such a variety of choices. Here a vinyl sheet flooring provides color wall to wall, and you never have to send it to the cleaners! The main colors of the flooring are picked up in walls, ceilings, and upholstery, providing decorative unity all through the house. Bright potted flowers seem to say "Follow me" as they mount the stairs into the living room.

Shh! You're surrounded by cork! Natural colors and textures never seem to lose their appeal. In favor for generations, they're still as desirable as ever. We're speaking of characteristics such as the subtle graining of walnut, the rough-gentle touch of tweed, the mellow warmth of cork. In this living room, with its unusual reading alcove, the generous use of cork has a purpose more than decorative. The cork tile flooring is quiet underfoot because of its natural resilience. And it's comfortable to walk on. The walls also are covered with squares of lightweight cork. This carries out the decorative theme and makes the whole space glow invitingly. The room appears to be designed for study, for reading, for letter writing. But do you know what? Guests love it, too.

When you'd like a larger living room. Almost any home can be updated with well-planned remodeling and redecorating. Look past the obvious, and interesting possibilities pop out of the shell. See that dining room off to the side of this living room? It was once a porch. But the family found that the living room was too cramped because of its eat-in area. They decided to do something about that. So they opened the wall (not difficult, because in this instance about all they had to do was remove a set of French doors) and "took in" the porch by enclosing it. Once this space had become part of the house interior, all sorts of new design opportunities emerged. A floor of sheet linoleum running from room to room makes the new area harmonize with the old. The family is pleased with the result and with its selection of an Oriental theme for the now-expanded space.

The living room that moved to the garden. As a family grows bigger, the living room often seems to grow smaller. This is especially true if a corner of it serves as your dining room. Here the space problem was solved when the family said, "Okay, dining room. You win." The old living room was turned into an honest-to-goodness dining room. And the new living room? It was built in the garden, right by the back steps. It's now a bright and lively room for family activities. The flooring, which can be installed by do-it-yourselfers, is of a vinyl-content tile in two patterns resembling natural cork. The wall on the far side of the room includes a slanted shelf for the display of magazines, an idea borrowed from the public library. And, because favorite books tend to become worn and shabby as they're read over and over, these bookshelves have pull-down shades to keep them out of sight when they're not in use.

Queen Victoria would have loved it. This living room and adjoining dining room illustrate how you can place your period furniture in a modern setting and achieve beautiful results. The Victorian settee and chairs have been uphostered in a festive fabric that makes the house fairly sparkle with life. The dining room features a chandelier that serves as an unusual but workable contrast to the late-nineteenth-century pieces. In one quiet corner of the living room is a reading nook, with a desk for letter writing. Speaking of quiet, the flooring of cork tile has a timeless quality about it that spans the years between traditional and contemporary and unites both styles in one decorative effect. Cork's natural resilience hushes the sound of footfalls. That's important for a living room that sometimes serves as a music room in this home.

When you want your home to speak "early American." In this comfortable house, the furnishings are intended to complement the Colonial theme. The cobbler's bench used as a coffee table, the high-back Windsor chair warming itself at the fireside, the quilted cover on the sofa, all contribute to the effect. But the room also contains certain modern touches that are practical and inexpensive and shouldn't be overlooked. The carpet, for instance. It's a springy blend of kraft fiber and wool-rayon-acetate yarns. The random color is woven clear through so the carpet is reversible for as much as twice the wear.

A fireplace wall with more than beauty. When it's glowing with warmth, a fireplace almost always takes center stage in a room. Even in the summertime, it's a large and important decorating element—though sometimes, to be frank, it represents wasted space when there's no fire. Here's one way to make a fireplace wall work a little harder: build in storage space. In this living room the designer found room for shelves, drawers, and cupboards. The television set can be hidden by a pull-down screen when not in use. The color scheme is neutral and restrained, so the flickering firelight can still be the star. A woven fiber carpet in a bamboo tone carries the quiet coloration to every corner of the room.

Inspired by a daydream of the South Sea. Decorating ideas may come from any corner of the map. A magazine article about the South Pacific led to this one. It brings the exciting leisure life of Hawaii right into the living room. Its lines are crisp and sheer, and this ideally fits the beachside setting. Important extra touches come from the accessories, chosen with care. The fireplace is flanked by a pan all ready for stir-frying and a wind-twisted branch that's set into a homemade holder. An abacus adds a decorative touch (and practical, too, if you know how to use one). Bamboo wind-chimes just outside the door bring music into the room day and night. Note especially the Oriental good-luck symbols set into the rubber tile flooring. A smooth-surface floor like this makes sense at the shore, as tracked-in sand sweeps away promptly. Please pass the pineapple!

Excitement on the bias. Artists often use slashing diagonal lines in their paintings to add vivacity and excitement. Offbeat angles and surprising corners perform the same magic in this living room. Begin with the flagstoned patio garden, thrusting right into the room. The unusual cut of the carpet and the angled placement of the couch at left point your eye past the patio to the modern dining room beyond. The kinetic action suggested by the wire sculpture stands for the busy, interested people who live in this home. The floor is an integral part of the decorative scheme. A colorful mosaic design inlaid in a gentle beige background provides individuality to the overall design. It's a sensible choice in flooring, because it's a vinyl-content tile that was selected for simple maintenance. The small tables can be moved quickly into place when guests arrive.

A room with a past gets a new chance. You should have seen this room a couple of weeks ago. It was shabby and outdated, as rooms in fifty-eight-year-old houses often are. The most pressing need was for a new floor. The drab wooden floor was coming apart at the seams and was badly stained. A new floor of linoleum sheet material was the starting point for all that followed to transform this room into a beauty spot any homeowner could be proud of. It was installed with a minimum of seams. And its soft, warm colorings and smart tone-on-tone textured effect immediately brought new life to the room. See how it harmonizes the contemporary furnishings with the room's original Victorian features, how it sets off the rug. The mirror over the mantel gives the illusion of more spaciousness by reflecting the room's features—and a room this handsome deserves to be repeated!

A color scheme that's easy to change. It can be surprisingly simple to change a room's appearance for winter and summer. The trick is to start with the largest decorating elements, the walls and floors. For these use soft "background" tones that harmonize with a variety of colors. Then, with a quick change of slip covers and other design elements, you can give the room an entirely new look. This living room is set to welcome wintertime guests for a light, casual lunch. But change to gray-blue slip covers and accessories (see inset) and the color scheme goes cool for summer. Soft, quiet colors for floors and walls are right for a home like this, and there are so many to choose from. Here the flooring is easy-to-clean vinyl-content tile in a subtle gray that goes with any color you please. Feature strips set into the floor add decorative interest.

When you don't have money to burn. Almost any young couple could find something to like about this living room. It's attractively fitted out, and with ideas that don't bludgeon the budget. Ample storage space is built into the bookshelf wall. In additon to the cupboards along the floor, the screens on either side of the television open to reveal more shelves at left and a set of drawers at right. The

furniture, including a simple coffee table and chairs with woven seats and backs, is comfortable but not costly. The beauty of nature is brought into the room through a glass door that opens into a garden and with an inexpensive potted fern added to the interior. The fiber rug is in a tweedy texture that blends well with other furnishings. This type of rug is reversible for extra beauty and extra wear.

When you don't mind spending to achieve true luxury.
There may never have been a flooring in all the world that
could do as much to show off really fine furnishings as this
one. It glows with the beauty of imported cork. But wait a
minute. Does cork have the stamina to hold up under
conditions of hard usage? This cork does. Its particles are
sealed under a wear layer of crystal-clear vinyl. The result

is a flooring you actually can look down into, a rich, deep-
textured effect in natural colorings. It's an opulent background for precious rugs and distinguished furniture. The
openwork screens reveal the furnishings, at least partially,
even from the patio garden of this home. Its elegance is
further suggested by the manteltop candelabra and the
spray of fresh flowers nearby.

Opposite top:

Indulge a taste for the modern, even on a budget. Some people like to listen to old favorites on phonograph records made years ago. When it comes to their homes, on the other hand, they want to be surrounded by an up-to-the-minute interior. In this living room we can find ideas for modern living that can be enjoyed even by those on a limited budget. Several of the accessories are treasures that, frankly, were expensive: the hand-carved screen, the antique decorated box on the mantel, the imported Oriental drawings. Once these items take their places, the room can be decorated around them without sending the homeowners into a "where will the money come from?" panic. The furniture is inexpensive though comfortable. Andirons like these can be picked up at a yard sale or auction. And the rug is a fiber weave that offers rich, tweedy colors but costs much less than most types of rugs.

A ceiling that soaks up noise. A gently moving mobile sculpture directs your eye toward the ceiling. So does the marbleized obelisk of a fireplace. That's all right, because in this balcony living room the ceiling is an important decorative feature. It's a lot more than just decorative, though. Applied on the underside of the balcony (foreground) and between the exposed beams, acoustical ceiling tiles absorb much of the noise that strikes them. Tiny openings in the textured surface of the ceiling soak up irritating household noises. This changes the racket of children, the buzz of appliances, and the jangling of telephones into an acceptable hum of family activity. Acoustical ceiling materials like this can be installed by a do-it-yourselfer.

Where did all those butter-flies come from? They're not real, of course. But the stylized butterfly motif is repeated in a couple of the elements of this handsome living room. The vinyl-content flooring in two patterns has insets made from a third color. The designs climb the fireplace wall in random placements, creating a decorative unity in the room. You can understand why dinner guests like to move into this room for their dessert. It fairly sings with invitation. Like the rest of the home interior, the stairway is bright and open. That makes it easier to appreciate the beauty of the plants and flowers in the garden just beyond the large window wall. The painting above the fireplace is mounted off-center for added visual interest.

Chapter 4

Bedrooms

Possibly the bedroom is the place in which we may most freely exercise our own personal decorating tastes. It offers boundless opportunities for creative expression. Armstrong shows the way with theme bedrooms (as an illustration, those designed especially for boys or for girls), bedrooms that can readily change appearance as the children grow older, bedrooms that can be used as sewing rooms or reading rooms, and bedrooms that exemplify luxurious living.

Who'd believe a room this fancy for so little cost? It was a serviceable but rather ordinary-looking room before (see inset), with furniture bought before the children were born. Now they're both nearing college age, and there's not a lot of bounce in the family budget. The redecorated room is full of clever surprises that you have to look twice to see. The big old chiffonier was sawed right through the middle. Now it's *two* bedside chests. The bed was turned around, end for end. The old headboard was sawed off down to the legs, and the old footboard became a smart low headboard. A long piece of plywood turned the little old vanity into a real dressing table. Decorators call the flowers on the walls and chests "découpage," but they're just cutouts from old wallpaper and picture books, pasted on and varnished. Everything's so flouncy, you'd think laundering it would be a chore. No, the swags and bedspread are shirred together with cords; they can just be pulled out, and then everything can be laundered flat. It may also take a second look to realize that the floor is made of linoleum, with embossing to give it a carved effect.

Begin with a bed and three barrels. A pair of newlyweds gulped when faced with the costs of furnishing their first house together. They were sensible, though. They decided not to spread their money too thin but to buy good things that would last even if they had to wait for other things. So they gave the bedroom of their home a floor of durable linoleum in a splatterdash effect that would complement the surroundings even if they decided to change the color scheme later. They had a bed. And they had three barrels, the barrels their wedding gifts had been packed in for the move to their new home. A bit of home carpentry work turned two of the barrels into chairs and the third into two hassocks. The bride found a lively flowered chintz for the upholstering. When she discovered that she could buy the rest of the bolt at a bargain price, she used it on one wall, too. Instead of building in a big wardrobe closet, as originally planned, the couple saved money with curtain-covered shelves. Pull the curtains and the shelves are right in front of you (see inset). Close the curtains, and they're hidden away.

A do-It-yourself project. Really. You don't nood a lot of money. You don't need a lot of talent. Imagination and daring? Well, yes, those help when you tackle a project like this. But every big idea in the room is one that do-it-yourselfers can handle. Take the dressing table. It started with two unpainted chests and a piece of plywood. The top drawer of each chest was cut off to make the two bedside tables. No legs are needed, because they're simply bolted to the wall. Putting on the chintz was easier than painting. It just took scissors and paste. The four-poster bed was made from porch posts; they're fastened to floor and ceiling. The curtain was staggered by hanging half of it from a ceiling track. That "chest" at the foot of the bed is a sewing cabinet. It has a double top, and that gives you twice as much work space (see inset). When sewing is finished, drop the top, close the doors, and everything is out of sight. Threads and snippings clean up with one swish of the dust mop because the floor is smooth-surface linoleum.

For a lady who loves a luxurious bedroom. This room blossomed from one that offered nothing more than four bleak walls, a small window, and a single closet. Now look at it. Some practical changes started with the addition of a closet. Not the ordinary kind that looks like an afterthought, but one that was planned to be an unobtrusive part of the decoration. It's concealed behind the wallpapered plywood panel at the head of the bed. Two rolling racks were specially designed to fit into either end of the closet shell. An easy pull brings all the clothes into full view (see inset). Valances were added as a foil for the soft flowing draperies. Extra-wide pale blue curtains made the small window seem larger and provided a background for the expansive dressing table. Full-length mirrors at either end of the closet give the room an illusion of spaciousness. The stylized leaves in the linoleum floor are embossed into its surface.

A master bedroom redone with class. Through renovation, this room was salvaged from one that had grown out-of-date and uninviting (inset 1). And all the furniture in it was reclaimed from the attic and basement! The bed, for instance, became stylish again after the footboard was cut down and the ornate headboard was painted to blend in with the wallpaper. Ancient coal-stove ornaments were wired to make bed lamps. A little 1890 office chair came out of retirement to become the blue velvet vanity seat. Now there's a place for everything. Behind the sliding doors on the storage wall are lots of hanging space and built-in drawers (inset 2). The man's bureau at the center of the side wall is loaded with space for shirts, socks, and ties. It's made from the drawers of an old chifforobe cut in half, stacked back to back, and topped off with plywood.

1

2

In a teen-age girl's room, glamor on a budget.
Wallpaper, paint, old furniture and new flooring can work miracles even when the budget dollars are tight. In this room for a teen-ager, the smart French bed was made from old twin headboards. The "chicken-wire" wallpaper is inexpensive. So is the long dressing table, which can be built by anyone who's handy with tools. Above the dressing table is a tackboard for prom invitations, photographs of favorite friends, and other mementos. A scroll-cut valance has a painted design that repeats the rooster theme. The room had been out-of-date and uninviting (inset 1). Then it got a drenching of fresh decorating ideas, such as the addition of twin fitted closets (inset 2). A new floor of linoleum promises simplified clean-ups for the busy occupant of the room.

1

2

For boys, a bunkhouse bedroom. Here's a room that accommodates two active youngsters and leaves them plenty of room to play. It's filled with space-saving, work-saving ideas that could be adapted for many a home. Arranging the bunks at right angles is unorthodox. But doing so makes room for a clothes closet and bookshelves with storage bins underneath, and it prevents a bumped head when the lower bunk is made up. Keeping the room neat is unusually easy, too. Toys are stored out of sight in the two handy bins. The floor of linoleum can be swept clean in a jiffy, because dust and dirt can't get a grip on its smooth, almost seamless surface. Linoleum in a different pattern covers the tops of the storage chests. Adjustable bed lamps and a clever light tree (see inset) provide plenty of light for young eyes. Model planes, which could clutter up the room, are pinned up out of the way on a giant cork bulletin board.

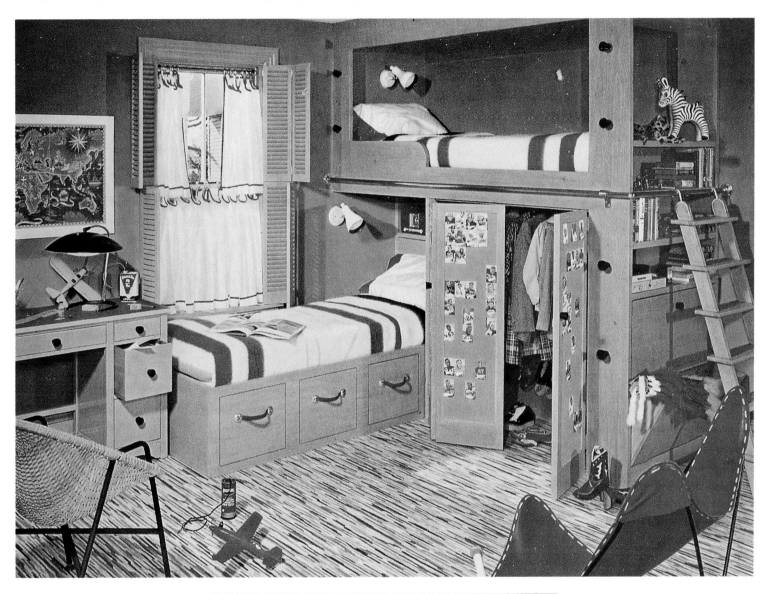

A room that grows up with your boys. It's fun to decorate a room for youngsters. Trouble is, children get older. Then what? A happy solution is a room like this one that can grow up as they do. When they're little, boys like to sleep under the "big top." A striped tent effect is achieved with plywood valances that are easy to remove a few years down the road. The clown feet on the beds are also made of plywood and can be taken off when the beds are refinished. The "circus rings" are inset into the linoleum floor. When the boys start reading adventure stories and collecting high school pennants, it takes only a few minor alterations to adapt the room to their new interests (see inset). The toy cabinets are transformed into bookcases and storage space. Beds, cabinets, and chest are refinished in wood tones, and the canvas-top toy table is replaced by a grown-up desk and chair. Walls and ceiling, now minus the valance, are painted to harmonize with the flooring, which is still good for many more years of service.

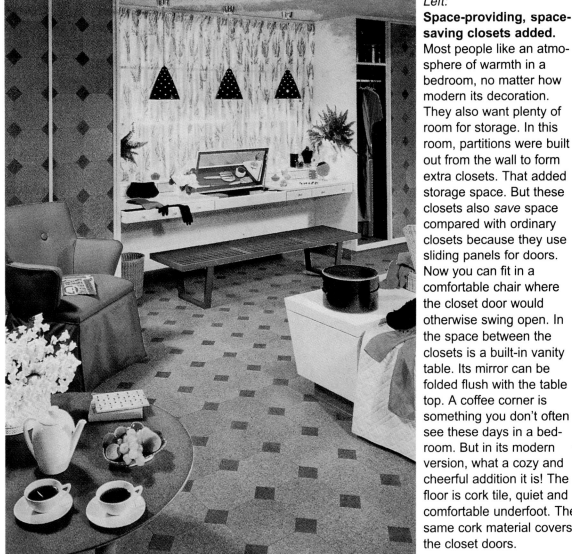

Above:

An overseas statement in American decorating.
Today, as fast travel and communication bring the ends of the earth closer together, you see new influences in American decorating that originate in the farthest corners of the world. It's a broad concept of interior design, one that offers lots of room for individuality without any sacrifice in comfort or livability. In this room, the furnishings are spare and uncomplicated. Yet they are combined with great style to suggest its Oriental origins. The hanging lanterns, positioned for bedtime reading, can be individually controlled. Overlapping pillows in alternating colors add decorating interest during daytime hours. Accessories, including potted ferns and philodendrons, interrupt the room's sheer straight lines. The whole effect is nicely framed by a linoleum floor and a beamed ceiling.

Left:

Space-providing, space-saving closets added.
Most people like an atmosphere of warmth in a bedroom, no matter how modern its decoration. They also want plenty of room for storage. In this room, partitions were built out from the wall to form extra closets. That added storage space. But these closets also *save* space compared with ordinary closets because they use sliding panels for doors. Now you can fit in a comfortable chair where the closet door would otherwise swing open. In the space between the closets is a built-in vanity table. Its mirror can be folded flush with the table top. A coffee corner is something you don't often see these days in a bedroom. But in its modern version, what a cozy and cheerful addition it is! The floor is cork tile, quiet and comfortable underfoot. The same cork material covers the closet doors.

Signing up color to be on your team. Sometimes decorating problems, even difficult problems, can be solved with a simple idea. As often as not, that idea revolves around the use of color. And color can work near-miracles. It can let you blend traditional furniture into a modern setting. It can help you make old rooms new. It can bring vitality to a room that is in danger of seeming too large, too unconnected. Take this room, with its high ceiling. How would you approach its interior design? You might start with the flooring, the largest single decorative element in the room, and let its color set the pace for the remainder of the room. Hey, that works! Now that color has been enlisted to be an important part of the team, we can look for ways to use it intelligently. Repeating the drapery fabric in upholstery, for example. And contrasting the light coloring of the floor with dark-finished wooden furniture.

But the head of the bed is not against the wall! An exciting concept in interior design is that today you can break out of the routine. You can take a fresh approach to color, to style, even to furniture arrangement. Why should the head of the bed always be against the wall? Why shouldn't you awaken in a shower of cool morning sunlight, filtered through a bamboo screen? And why shouldn't you go barefoot when the touch of a cork tile floor is so comfortable underfoot? The screen separates the sleeping area from one that can be used for dressing, reading, or quiet conversation. On either side of the screen, counterweighted light fixtures move up or down at a touch. Figurines, lacquerware, and other accessories lend a touch of the Far East to this comfortable, practical American interior.

Look what's new upstairs. It's that refreshing "downstairs look" of spaciousness and livability you find in so many homes nowadays. Here it's achieved with a bold sweep of texture and color, carried from room to room in the vinyl sheet flooring. Though the flooring has the appearance of a mesh weave, its suface is actually smooth and easy to keep clean. It's a sheet material, so there are few seams (you'll have to look hard to find them in this design!). The room offers unusual design elements, such as the strongly vertical screen and the lush gathering of tassels at the corners of the bed. It's appealing enough that you want to spend some of your leisure hours here—in reading, for example. Sprays of fresh flowers help to make it beautiful, and all that storage space helps to make it practical.

A motel room that really does look like home. When you turn in at a motel's "no vacancy" sign, you like the feeling that you're going to meet a friendly, inviting atmosphere, inside as well as out. Here's a motel room that wants you to feel as welcome as in your own home. To begin with, it offers lots of storage room for your suitcases, your clothes, and your toilet articles. And you have space on the countertops for writing letters or reports. Fold-away racks support suitcases but can be quickly stowed when not in use. A whimsical map mural recognizes that "we're all travelers here." The durable flooring of asphalt tile extends into the bath for decorative unity. Heavy drapes behind the bank of plants shield the wayfarers from light when they're ready to turn in.

It takes a bit of brass. Also lace, velvet, and cork. But look at the result. Here's a room so appealing that you might want to sleep late, then stay even longer. Flanking the oversize bed are lamps that stand atop tables loaded with reading material. A desk with a fold-down shelf is ready for letter-writing, and its velvet-covered chair assures comfort. A window that bends around the corner lets in lots of light, gently filtered through the lace curtains. Cork is a good choice for the floor of a bedroom. It looks so luxuriously warm and comfortable; and it feels that way, even to bare feet. As an added touch of elegance in this room, hollow diamonds of brass with centers of gleaming white vinyl are set right into the cork tile floor. That adds drama to the overall effect.

For two girls several years apart in age. Would you believe that sisters of different ages could share one bedroom and get along in almost perfect harmony? This bedroom lets them do just that. The key is the removable partition, which gives them privacy to pursue their separate interests. That makes it like having two individual bedrooms in one space. Yet the interior has a unified look because it is decorated with care. Each part has the same wallpaper, the same area rugs, the same type of wicker furniture. Spatter linoleum extends into each. And resilient flooring like this has a practical appeal for both of the room's occupants. If the younger sister spills the teen-ager's face powder during a growing-up moment, she can quickly wipe away the evidence from this floor's smooth, almost seamless surface.

You step down into this bedroom. An unusual bedroom is filled with treasures gathered from faraway places. Its beauty is enhanced by the dramatic act of moving down three stairs each time you enter it. Lamps and lighting fixtures of several types highlight the combination of furniture that ranges from richly carved imported pieces to a Victorian chair. The bed is low, covered in a fabric suggestive of batik. In the dressing table, storage space is made abundant because of the arrangement of drawers of various sizes. The flooring is intriguing because it actually has depth. You can look down into it. Tiny squares of vinyl, thousands and thousands of them, are held in place by a transparent vinyl grout. The overall effect is that of expensive hand-laid mosaic tiles.

Opposite bottom:
Black and white and practical all over. The black-and-white look makes fashion news year in and year out. The reason is that it makes such an ideal background for colorful furnishings and accessories in the home, especially when it is used with large-scale decorating elements. In this room the flooring is a mosaic effect in vinyl sheet form. Because it's essentially a black-and-white pattern, it makes a pleasant background for rugs and goes with any color. That opens up a broad range of decorating possibilities. The floor-level trim on the poster bed is repeated at the ceiling. Comfortable chairs and a round coffee table make this a room for leisure-time relaxing. After all, if you're fortunate enough to have a fireplace in your bedroom, you may as well make the most of it.

A teen-age girl gets her very own room. And her own telephone! And even her own bathroom next door! For any girl reaching the age at which privacy is of looming importance, a room like this would be the realization of a dream. She has a well-lighted desk; and that provides a place for homework, so it no longer has to use up space at the dining room table. Latticed dividers set off the bed and the window above. There's room for a Victorian doll house, a treasured carryover from younger days. Furnishings are chosen to encourage the teen-age occupant to keep this room neat. For instance, the fitted bed cover goes into place with hardly more than a flip. And the linoleum flooring swishes clean with an occasional damp-mopping. The room is quiet, too, because its acoustical ceiling absorbs a lot of the noise that's generated when friends come over.

Chapter 5

Bathrooms

Must the bathroom, that most functional of rooms, be only utilitarian? The illustrations in this chapter suggest otherwise. They show how the application of imagination and decorative wit—sometimes with the added touch provided by do-it-yourself skills—can turn the humble bathroom into a space that can hold its own with any area of the home. And these bathrooms not only are appealing in appearance; they also are designed for easy care.

It's a powder room—and also the family bath. When they come into this attractive powder room, guests may not realize that it serves the family as its bathroom. Where's the rack of toothbrushes, the soggy washcloth on the tub, the row of half-empty prescription bottles? Where's the feeling of invading someone else's privacy when you enter the room? Like most one-bathroom houses, this one suffered all those faults. Then it was done over, and just a couple of inexpensive steps made a real difference. First, a curtain was hung to hide the old-fashioned bathtub and to separate the family's part of the room from that used by guests. Second, a linoleum floor, individualized with contrasting feature strips, was installed to add new life to the room. Now when the curtain is opened (see inset) it's the familiar family bath. When the curtain is closed, it's an up-to-date powder room. And few guests realize that the room serves double duty.

Did they have bathrooms like this in colonial days?
They probably would have if they could have. If a home's architecture is colonial in style, why not make the bathroom interior colonial also? It's simple to do, as this room shows. An arm chair rests on a braided rug. An antique mirror stand is on the dressing table. Lamps and lighting fixtures suggest the period. A turned wooden post dresses the corner of the cabinets that serve as a room divider.

The hardware is wrought iron in a design frequently found in homes of the colonial time. And a folk art angel above the dressing table provides another touch of Early America. Linoleum in a splatterdash design completes the picture. Kitchens and bathrooms are what sell houses. When the homeowners decide it's time to sell their house, don't you think they'll find it easier to sell with this room than if it had an *ordinary* bathroom?

For people who hate scrubbing bathrooms. All bathrooms need cleaning from time to time, and this one is no exception. But it does have a special feature or two worth noting. The smooth-surface resilient floor doesn't offer much traction for dirt. It cleans up with a pass of a damp mop. The flooring is coved up the sides of walls and partitions to eliminate dirt-catching corners. Walls and even the ceiling are coated with a similar material, available in big sheets that can be quickly cemented over the old walls. The vanity table and the lavatory are up off the floor, so it's easy to clean beneath them. And the bright primrose yellow that establishes the color scheme looks lustrous and bright always.

A bath with a view. It's a small window, admittedly; but it overlooks a pleasant vista, so why not make use of it? There's no reason a bathroom should "keep its eyes closed" any more than another room in the house. Here the window can remain open to the light most hours of the day. When privacy is desired, a pull-down curtain does the trick. The toilet area can be separated from the rest of the room by another curtain, near the built-in dressing table. For easy maintenance, walls and ceilings are covered with a tile that's made of porcelain fused onto a base of steel. Wiping once in a while with a damp cloth keeps it clean.

Making two rooms out of one. Many a house built in the 1950s had just one bathroom. And, because of the basic box design of the house, there was no sensible or inexpensive way to add a powder room. This room was once an outdated family bath (see inset). Now it has been renovated to become an attractive powder room and a practical bathroom, too. The first step was to get rid of that bathroom look. A specially cut inset in the new linoleum flooring was like a path to the door, and that helped. So did a wallpaper panel that pictured a tropical beach seen through half-opened shutters. The unpleasant-looking parts of radiator, lavatory, and bathtub were covered up; new cabinets were added, and a spiffy dressing table replaced the old-fashioned one. Built-in lighting, hidden behind valances, gives plenty of illumination. Now guests enjoy using the powder room, and seldom do they even think about this as the family's bath.

Does it take a woman to plan a pretty bathroom?
Maybe so. In any event, a woman did this one. It's more than pretty, though, as it contains a number of practical ideas that could be incorporated into the planning stage for almost any home. To begin with, the tub and toilet were placed back to back, with the shower wall in between. That saved money by keeping the pipes together. Then it made sense to put the washbowl near the other fixtures. It's

attached to a little wall at the end of the tub, and that forms a sort of alcove for the toilet. The alcove can be completely closed off by a draw curtain. With the fixtures tucked away, there was room for a good-sized wrought-iron dressing table and chair. The chintz is a lily of the valley print, and a matching design was painted on the edge of the mirror that's over the washstand. On the floor, a scallop border was cut to fit the design of the embossed linoleum.

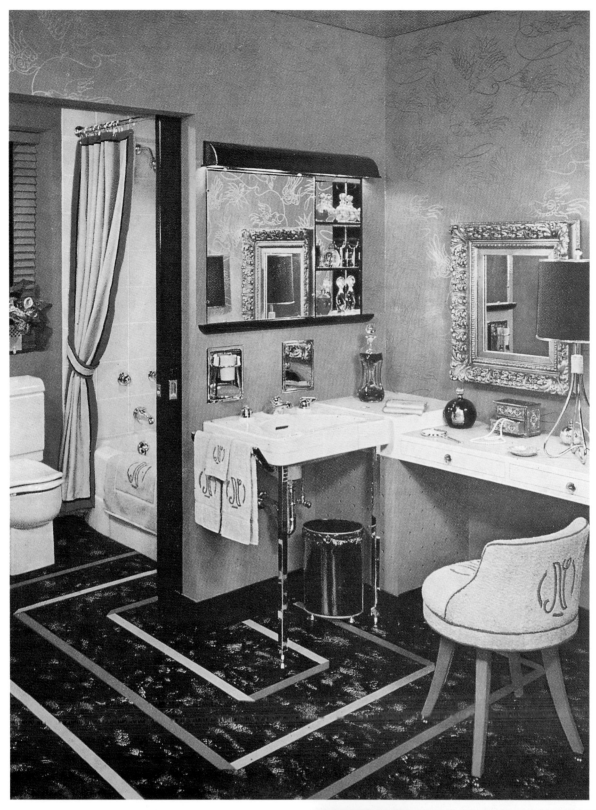

No extra fixtures, no extra plumbing. A powder room added to the home can quickly double bathroom costs. But here's a room that incorporates the advantages of a powder room right in the family bath, with little or no added expense. The idea struck like a thunderbolt when a young couple were looking over the plans for the house they wanted to build. No extra money to put in a powder room, they agreed, but at least they would have one big bathroom. Then it hit them. Hey! We can have the powder room just by including a wall partition by the side of the tub. The basin could be moved to the powder room side, they realized; that meant no additional fixtures or plumbing would be needed. A sliding door closes to hide the bathroom area (see inset). A special geometric design set into the linoleum floor adds depth to the room. The monogram on the back of the dressing table chair is repeated in towels and bath mat.

One bathroom in a house for four people. Mom, Dad, and two daughters all have to share this bathroom. How does it manage to look so much like an attractive powder room? The secret is in the L-shaped partition, which gives everyone some privacy. Dad doesn't like to have his daughters peering over his shoulder when he's at the lavatory, shaving. So for the girls they put a dressing table and extra mirror on the other side of the partition. This becomes the center of attention in the room, and now you hardly notice the rest of the fixtures. Sometimes a partition can make a room look awfully cut up. But they've thought of a solution to that one, too. A linoleum floor ties the whole room together decoratively, and its stripes running across the room make it look wider. Working out the color scheme was simple, because the colors are picked up from those in the flooring.

The "no-wasted-motion" bathroom. In some small bathrooms, you can find yourself bumping into the walls or bumping into yourself. You always feel cramped and crowded. Not so here. The fixtures are arranged efficiently, with storage space right at hand. It's a step-saver. It's a maintenance-saver, too. The walls are covered with a glass-smooth finish that just can't hold dirt. And it resists acids, soap, medicines, sunlight and even hard knocks. Joints and edges are finished with a bright metal trim. On the floor, the rectangle set into the linoleum makes the room appear larger and also reflects the sheer, trim lines of the cabinets and other furnishings.

No crowding here. Here's a bathroom that comfortably accommodates two people at the same time. It's a renovation of a dingy, old-fashioned bathroom in an older house (inset 1). In the updated version, the lady of the house has her own pretty vanity-washstand topped with triple mirrors. A separate lavatory replaces the old undersized basin and gives the man a place to shave and store his toiletries. Plumbing bills were kept at a minimum by re-using old pipelines, and that left room in the budget for a new shower-tub combination (center background, inset 2). The window shutters are made from metal mesh designed for radiator covers. This novel treatment gives privacy yet plenty of light, and it eliminates the need for curtains that have to be washed and ironed. The unusual towel and magazine racks are another original touch. Who'd guess that they were made by simply welding rods to old Victorian keyhole escutcheons?

1

2

Nine years of dreaming went into this bath. The couple who built this home had lived in several places before. And in the nine years of their marriage, in all those places, the wife had never really been satisfied with the bathroom. When it came time to build their dream house, she knew what she wanted: a bath as well-planned as the other rooms in the home. The beginning of the elegance she had yearned for was the diamond design in the linoleum floor, which is coved up the base of the wall to eliminate corners where dirt and water collect. Because a stall shower and a roomy dressing table were other luxuries she had longed for, she carried out the diamond theme in the special shower door and the cabinet trim at the ends of the dressing table. The shower door, L-shaped, folds back when not in use; that enables the stall shower to be incorporated within the conventional tub. This is a bathroom with lots of cabinets and shelves. Extra drawers are built around the washbowl, and a bench-like shelf with a hinged cover camouflages the toilet.

The beauty of a home needn't stop at the bathroom door. Are you one of those homemakers who has a sinking feeling when anyone outside the family heads for your bathroom? Here's how imaginative decoration can bring beauty to this sometimes neglected room. Style was ushered in with colorful chintz. The flower motif around the mirror was cut from the same chintz used on the wall in the toilet alcove, and its pattern inspired the room's closely harmonized color scheme. A step up to the tub makes bath time safer for youngsters and gives Mom a place to sit while scrubbing small ears. Garment pegs at the alcove entrance (see inset) are placed at convenient heights for the little ones in the family. They're right next to a chart to measure the children's growth over time. The curved dressing table, with its splashproof plastic laminate top, provides plenty of space. Additional storage room is built into the wall of the alcove.

More than just a bathroom. The feeling of spaciousness that you find in some of today's homes can be the result of combining several rooms—such as bathroom, dressing room, and bedroom—into one open area. In this home, the combination works efficiently and conveniently. Frosted windows alongside the sunken tub provide privacy while letting in plenty of light. The curtains may be drawn at night to darken the room for sleep. Counter space at the lavatory is ample, and the dressing table provides room for a layout of accessories that are used frequently. Both lavatory and dressing table are equipped with large mirrors. Sliding screens partially shield the bathing area from the bedroom. To treat such a multipurpose room as one single decorative unit, with continuity of color and design, a floor of linoleum has been installed throughout.

Tub or stall shower? Why not both? Every family has its own ideas as to what makes a perfect bathroom. Some people insist on stall showers. Others are confirmed tub addicts. When this bath was planned, both were included. It turned out to be a special blessing because it adds efficiency when the family is large. A rack of towels is situated between the tub and the shower, with a sliding door to hide it when it's not in use. Another sliding door provides privacy for the toilet alcove. Double sinks are a great convenience for brothers who are both rushing to get ready for school. Recessed lighting fixtures over the lavatories augment the natural light that pours through the skylight. The room is large enough to include a sunlamp and tanning couch. The vinyl sheet flooring is installed in a special mitered-corner design to give the appearance of even more space.

A bathroom that takes in washing. It's far more than just a bathroom. It's a complete laundry center, too, with a washer-dryer, ironing table, and ample linen storage. A good-looking room, but it's a work-saver, too. The built-in partition has open shelves for towels, so they're accessible from either the tub or the lavatory side. Just above the counter is a sizable window, with curtains that can be drawn for privacy. Near at hand is a rack for magazines, for those who come to stay a few minutes. The partition does more than separate the toilet alcove from the rest of the room; it's also a storage wall. That's where the bath toys go, for example, when they're not being used. Easy maintenance was one of the considerations when this room was created. That's assured because the linoleum flooring cleans up with a swipe of a damp mop. The daisy-like designs are set right into the flooring for a fresh decorative touch.

Washable all the way. With small children in the family, you have a double reason for choosing home furnishings that offer easy-care opportunities. First, you want to be able to clean up dirt and spills readily. Second, you want to assure good hygiene in the home. This bathroom meets both criteria because it's plastic and washable, from the floor up. The wall covering, like the flooring, is made of a smooth, simple-to-clean plastic sheet material. Foldaway plastic curtains can be used to separate the various parts of the room. A step built into the lavatory cabinet makes it easier for youngsters to brush their teeth and develop other good personal habits. Near the tub, a tilt-out laundry hamper is a place for used towels. Sliding mirrors form the doors of the medicine cabinet. And a rack at the end of the counter keeps a bathroom glass handy for each member of the family.

Taking a fresh approach to color. What's that old style rule? "Blue and green should never be seen"? This bathroom demonstrates how outmoded that idea is. It shows how you can use color more freely than you may have imagined, without worrying about rules somebody may have made up in the past. The room has other fresh ideas, too. The twin sinks, for example, are separated by the bathtub that sticks out from the wall so it can be entered from either side. On the far side of the room, the lavatory counter takes an L-bend and becomes a well-lighted dressing table. Sliding mirrors hide the contents of the medicine cabinets. The color scheme originates in the rubber tile flooring of two colors, with brass insets to provide highlights. And on the open rack that holds towels, even the glass soap container adds to the visual effect.

Remodeling to reach a dream. When you're renovating the bathroom of an older home, you may as well stretch your imagination and go all the way to the dream of a room you've always wanted. It may not be as difficult to achieve as you think. In this home, the large window dominating one wall seemed at first to set limits on the bathroom design. But when the window was used as a starting point, other elements fell into place naturally. Now it's the site for a dressing table, flanked by bathroom sink counters. The tub and shower stall are equipped with sliding glass doors. This is a room you'd want to spend time in, and there's space for a couch for reading and relaxing. In the linoleum flooring, the installer cut and fitted the inset rings so perfectly that hardly a speck of dust can slip between the seams. He curved the linoleum up the walls, too, to eliminate hard-to-clean corners.

A striking new look for an older bathroom. When a bathroom goes blah with age and you want to give it a powerful punch, consider a decorative approach like this. Essentially, there was nothing wrong with the bath in this home (see inset). Even the 25-year-old flooring was still in good condition, though out of style. The problem was that the room lacked spirit. Just look at it now, after a redo to give it a festive carnival atmosphere. Tasseled swags set off the vivid striped curtains that bring the room its character. The old lavatory has been replaced by a modern one, mounted in a cabinet that offers much-needed storage space. Set into the vinyl sheet flooring are vinyl circles in contrasting colors. And "helping hands" are all over the place, including the soap dish and the wall-mounted sconce.

A seaside setting far from the sea. If you can't spend all your time at the shore, much as you'd like to, here's a way to enjoy a seaside atmosphere anyway, every day. It's like luxurious littoral living, right in your own home. Real treasures garnered from the beach are used in appropriate places, such as in the cabinet door pulls and in the translucent dividing wall between tub and toilet alcove.

And the shell-and-starfish motif is echoed in towel racks, in embroidered bath mat and chair seat, and even in the stylized designs set into the vinyl sheet flooring. Pull-out shelves bring the telephone and other conveniences into easy reach, then slide back into hiding when they're no longer needed. An adjoining sun room with a couch is dressed in light that floods through its windows.

Chapter 6

Family rooms, recreation rooms, and dens

The addition of the family room to the American home in the years following World War II—a room that, by whatever name, was devoted to the various interests and activities of the family—represented an important change in the way people were spending their leisure hours. Armstrong's ads reflected the change and in many instances led it. In this chapter, watch for the special touches, such as the provision for extra storage space in unexpected places.

Noise not a problem here. When you're having fun in a room like this, there's bound to be some noise. The easy way to keep noise from becoming a problem is to install an acoustical ceiling. Such a ceiling has a perforated or fissured surface. That traps some of the sound that hits the ceiling and keeps it from bouncing around the room so it can grow into an irritating racket. The tile is manufactured with a washable white finish, and you can even repaint it without losing its high acoustical efficiency. A noise-absorbing ceiling like the one in this room is designed for installation by do-it-yourselfers. Here, a valance of scalloped fabric draws attention to the overhead surface. And why not? The ceiling is attractive as well as practical.

This den keeps its secret well. One of the easiest ways to provide extra sleeping space for your guests is to make one of the rooms in your home do double duty. If you design it carefully, no one is likely to suspect that your room has a second use. This den or family room, for example, is so luxurious looking and livable that few people would dream there's a guest bedroom with built-in vanity hidden away here. The raised fireplace, the hanging lights, and the simplicity of the furnishings have a lot to do with the room's air of elegance as a den. But pull out the lower sofa and presto! Now we see comfortable twin beds for overnight guests (see inset). One section of the window ledge can be raised to reveal the mirror of a vanity table. A floor of cork tile provides underfoot quiet and comfort, whatever use the room is being put to at the moment.

A spare room that's busy all the time. In an older home, a small room, only 13 feet by 13 feet, was converted into a family room that's unusually versatile. Originally it was a bedroom (inset 1). Then a partition and a few clever, space-saving ideas turned it into much more. Look at the couch, for example. Just the thing for a comfortable family room, right? But it's really two big hassocks that convert into comfortable twin beds when guests arrive. The woven headboards conceal the bedding, one of many features that keep this active room from feeling crowded. When the beds are hidden away, the room again becomes a den for all kinds of family activity (inset 2). The chessboard, inlaid in the top of the refinished table, lifts up to disclose a vanity compartment, complete with mirror. When the space becomes a sewing room (inset 3), down comes a sewing table, uncovering handy racks for thread and notions on the wall. Behind the center mirror is a built-in ironing board. The third mirror hides a closet for unfinished sewing and other odds and ends. Then it's back to a guest room (inset 4), with the luxury of a private bath for your overnight visitors.

1

2

3

4

Left:

A small room that fills two big needs. Here's a room just nine feet square. But it shows how you can have a television room for the family and a comfortable room for guests, even when you don't have a separate room to devote to each. One of the secrets of this double-duty room is the use of built-in cabinets that make the most of wall space and take up little floor area. Some of the cabinet space is devoted to storing such family articles as games and phonograph records; some is left empty for use by overnight visitors. With a mirror added, a desk converts into a dressing table. The bed folds back into the sofa once the guests depart. In a room this small, it's helpful to use decorative elements that suggest roominess. For example, the cork tile flooring is installed in a herringbone design that gives an illusion of greater width and length.

Below:

Would you call this a family room? Well, yes, because so much of the family's activity is centered in this area. It's clearly the central nervous system of this home. But it's more than just a family room. It combines kitchen, dining room and living room as well. The reason it's able to carry out so many functions is its open planning. Eliminating partitions, letting rooms flow into each other, using one big expanse of color on the floor— all can help make houses look larger than they actually are. So the area doesn't appear crowded even when different activities are going on at the same time. The vent for the kitchen range is set into the chimney tower for efficiency, as is the double oven. Everywhere you look, you find storage space, even just above the range. The linoleum flooring is accented by an area rug in a harmonizing color. The windows vent open for fresh air.

When you have space to grow. The family is expanding, and the house needs to expand with it. If you have space within the home that can be finished off as an added room, you're fortunate. Now the question is how to do that most effectively. The important thing is to achieve the same comfort and livability you enjoy in the remainder of the house and to avoid that bare "afterthought" look. This can be done whether you're tackling a basement room or, as here, an attic. Several ideas combine to make this an attractive family room that doubles as a guest room. One wall has been opened to create a spacious window. A free-standing wood stove, tied into the chimney of the home, adds the cheery warmth that a fireplace always provides. The flooring is cork tile, offering mellow, nut-brown tones and a rich texture underfoot.

A do-as-you-please room for all the family. When a family room is planned right, it's a room for *every* member of the family. This house was developed around such an area. The kitchen and dining room are part of it; so Mom isn't left out of things, even when she's getting meals. Storage space is well-positioned, with open cupboards on the floor that encourage the youngsters to put away their large rolling toys. Built into a corner, the fireplace spreads its warmth into dining area and family room alike. That helps to unify the decorative theme. So does the expanse of almost seamless linoleum. It's easy to keep clean, too. There may be chaos here at 5 P.M., with stepped-on crayons, cut-up bits of paper, or the usual trails of cookie crumbs. But it takes only minutes to give the room a fresh, spring-cleaned look, ready for an evening of family relaxation.

It takes little money to bring a room to life. A family room should be full of life, ripe with an invitation for the whole family to enjoy its activities together. It's possible to reinvigorate a dull and uninteresting space with the proper decoration, and you can do it without cutting into your children's inheritance! In this room, for example, see how inexpensive furnishings work together in harmony. Two coffee tables are butted together to form a more interesting arrangement along the wall. They, the sofa, and the hassock are available at low cost. And the fiber rug is about as bargain-priced as any rug can be. Yet it's attractive and practical, with a reversible feature that gives it up to twice the wear.

Family room by day, guest room at night.
Here's a room that's on duty twenty-four hours a day. It's an area for family activities most of the time, but it's ready to help out as a guest room when called upon. By day, there's no hint of the bedroom it hides. You can see at once that it's a wonderful spot for relaxation with an interesting book, a phonograph record, or a good television show. If it can be converted into a bedroom, though, where's the bed? Ah, there it is! Just pull out a drawer in the entertainment wall (see inset), and the space turns into a luxurious room for overnight guests. The curtains may be drawn for privacy, and pull-down lamps provide light for reading. The flooring has the warm, natural appearance of cork, but it's actually a cork-like effect in vinyl-content tile. A do-it-yourselfer can install a floor like this one, using scissors and a brush for tools.

Nothing to get in the way of fun. From a junior cowboy's morning gallop to the end of the grownups' late show, this versatile family room offers relaxation for everyone. And with no "Don't do that!" or "Careful, John!" to spoil the fun. From the swing suspended from the ceiling (and currently occupied by a bear) to the carousel horse, it's a room clearly intended for children to enjoy. It even has an authentic soda fountain in the corner. But it's a place for adults, too, especially because cleanups are simple after the children's play hours. The vinyl-content tile floor, with inset feature strips of a contrasting color, is easy to whisk dust-free with a damp mop. The room has an unusual feature that should be especially appealing to homemakers: a "mud closet" (see inset). When little feet track rainy-day residue indoors, the children's hats, coats and boots can be placed in this closet to drip dry.

Leisure-loving family room converts to dining room. Television set, record player, a library of books, comfortable furniture, all point to the diverse family activities that go on here. But after a busy day, the room converts in minutes to an elegant formal dining room (see inset). One secret is in the cabinet doors. They slide left and right to hide the bookcases and to reveal dinnerware. Something similar goes on in the lower cabinets, whose sliding doors cover the television set and phonograph. The floor looks for all the world like one of those rare old parquet floors. But it isn't. It's linoleum in two colorings of a wood-grain styling, and it sets off both the "characters" that the room takes on. When it's time for dining, the lamps on the light poles are turned upward, bouncing illumination from the ceiling for a soft indirect effect.

What would you like to do here? Here's a family room that welcomes almost any activity that a member of the family can think of, even if several different activities are going on at the same time. When it's a party room, its uncluttered good looks open the way to good times. When it's the children's playroom, the tough vinyl-content flooring tile can take the rough-and-tumble without showing a sign of wear. That's why the family can even dare to include a sandbox in the room. Spilled things wipe away from the smooth surface with a flick of a sponge mop. Inset strips, in four different colors, run across the width of the room to give it the illusion of more space. Despite its modern approach to living, the room makes use of reproductions of antique furnishings to suggest old-fashioned hospitality.

Opposite top:

Two small rooms and a dreary hallway? Used to be. Now it's a family room that young and old can enjoy. A striking transformation has taken place here, thanks to some daring decorating ideas. The ideas include ceiling beams that provide a bold accent where room partitions once were and an ingenious spiral staircase to save space. The built-in coffee bar has bookshelves above and sloped racks for magazines and favorite works of art. Folding tables are for snacks during television time, but they quickly snap out of sight when they're not needed. One of the room's special features is its acoustical ceiling. It provides a smart new appearance, and it quiets the room by soaking up much of the noise that strikes it. Goes nicely with the open-beam look, too.

Striking the right note. In some homes, family rooms take on added functions. They're used for all sorts of get-togethers, true, but they also serve various members of the family as hobby rooms or sewing rooms or artists' studios. In this house the family room is, at times, a music room. And how well designed it is for this purpose! The richly paneled fireplace wall adds a visual warmth even when there's no fire on the hearth. As you enter the room, you step down into it. Beneath the top platform is space for storing firewood and toys; and the platform itself serves as a small stage for musical recitals presented to family members and friends. The flooring provides a quiet beauty of its own. It's a vinyl sheet material with tiny squares of vinyl scattered at random within a clear grout, so it looks as though the little tiles may have been placed in by hand, individually.

Chapter 7

Converted "extra-space" rooms

Growing families with growing children may find that they need additional space. But building a new home or relocating to a different, larger house can be an expensive solution to the problem. As this chapter shows, the answer can come through creative exploration of the existing home. Basements, attics, side porches, even garages can be adapted to add beautiful rooms that meet the needs and the interests of every member of the family.

Ten minutes ago this basement was a playroom. In less time than it takes to put the youngsters to bed, this basement room can be converted from a children's playroom (see inset) to an inviting place for adult entertaining. Hide away the toys on the shelves behind the draperies, flip over the furniture cushions, and the transition is complete. The other room decorations serve equally well for child's or grown-up's recreation. A chess set, for example, is set into a niche to provide an interesting feature for the wall at right. Because the subfloor of a basement is concrete in direct contact with the ground, not every flooring material will do. But this room has a floor of asphalt tile, which well withstands the effect of alkaline moisture always present in such conditions.

No longer looks like a basement. An amazing transformation can take place when you turn your imagination loose on unused basement space and convert it to an added room for your home. See how a caterpillar of a basement (see inset) can be turned into a butterfly with a few clever ideas. Supporting columns become part of the decoration, especially with the addition of counters and cabinets. A framework for potted plants at left has the appearance of a window wall because of electric lighting behind its draperies. Banquette seating in the far corner offers a spot for casual dining or recreation. In a portion of the room, the concrete block wall is still visible, with its interesting texture; but it's been painted to become a part of the decorative scheme.

No "blue Mondays" allowed. It takes more than modern appliances to do away with washday blues. You need a cheerful place to work. In many a house, the basement provides the starting place for a laundry that is as fresh and inviting as any such workplace can be. Here we see how many possibilities are offered by a drab basement (see inset). The small, high window and the outside stairway were in place already. Now they've been brightened with potted geraniums and with the addition of a Dutch door to assure plenty of daylight. The old divided sinks are hidden by paneling and cupboards, as is the electrical box. At right is a lighted bar for hanging fresh-washed clothing, and a hamper on wheels is another washday convenience. A hutch for storage makes this a gardening room as well as a laundry room. New ceiling and flooring tiles complete the picture.

Climb the attic stairs for an added room. It was like adding a new multipurpose room to the house when the attic was remodeled. Now it can be, in turn, a playroom for the children, a home office for the parents, a sewing room, or a secluded homework getaway for the high-schooler. It even converts into a guest room, because the sofas on each side of the room can be quickly turned into double-deck bunks (see inset). Linens and blankets are stored in cabinets behind the sofas. For privacy, a bamboo screen is lowered from an overhead beam. Tucked into a dormer, there's a complete bathroom for friends who come into town for the horse show and stay overnight. The linoleum floor has a game design inset to add a special life to parties.

Hunting for extra space? Don't overlook the basement.
The outdoors types who own this home needed extra room. They found that, with a bit of creative thought, they could find space in their basement for a comfortable "hunting lodge" to be enjoyed by the whole family. The project began with a fireplace to match the one in the living room directly above. Walls were finished with a paneling that suggests a log cabin. Furnishings are unashamedly rustic, though comfortable. Built in at left is a serving bar, complete with simple kitchen appliances. Decoys and other outdoor-activity items become important decorating elements in this room. The floor, of asphalt tile, is set off with inexpensive die-cut insets that help carry out the theme.

Carved out of an attic corner. Wasted attic space can be turned into a cheerful extra bedroom, and it doesn't take that long to accomplish. Here an unused portion of the attic is well-utilized through a bit of planning and the proper selection of interior finishing materials. The bed fits nicely under the sloping ceiling. But a full-height vertical surface is at the foot of the bed; and that provides wall space for the dresser as well as room for a closet behind it. Draperies and a wooden valance are carried across two walls to extend the interior theme. One key to the room's effectiveness is the paneling, which decorates and also insulates against summer heat and winter cold. It goes up quickly over a wooden framework and is installed here both in the long "plank" form for walls and in "tile" sizes for the ceiling.

A small jewel of a basement family room. In this house, a dark and dusty basement was to be finished off as a laundry room. But then the homeowners realized that they could use a portion of the area for a small family room. And that's what they did. Now there's a television set down there, along with comfortable chairs and diffused lighting. It's a room for relaxing. The laundry room, beyond the stairway, doesn't interfere with the family's activities in this room. Asphalt tile provides a smooth flooring underfoot. The interior finish throughout is a fiberboard material with a factory-applied painted surface. It adds beauty to the basement project; and it simplifies heating problems because it provides insulating value, too.

Laundry or playroom? This basement is both. It's like magic the way this basement can be changed from the laundry to an inviting party room. Roll back the ironer, then close the curtains to hide the laundry appliances. All signs of washday have disappeared. Now a snack bar lifts out from a cupboard recessed in the wall (see inset), and just that quickly the room is ready for entertaining. The furnishings are serviceable and well suited to this room's double identity. But it's the floor of asphalt tile that makes it all so practical. Spills can be mopped up from its smooth surface without leaving a trace. Because the flooring is laid tile by tile, there's almost no limit to the variety of original designs that can be created. Here the basic field color is goldenrod, with accents of ebony in a marbleized effect. A metalwork valance provides decorative interest at the ceiling.

Adding a room for the home craftsman. Let's say that you're the kind of person who likes to make things with your hands. But it's difficult to find the proper place in the home to turn loose your creative instincts. One problem is that your work tends to make a mess, at least temporarily. Another is that sometimes you must leave in the middle of a project, and that means you need room for jobs in progress. The solution could be to turn your basement into a workshop. This one provides an orderly arrangement of equipment, along with a cheerful atmosphere to work in. Handy shelves hold how-to-do-it manuals. Tools are stored ready at hand along the walls. There's even a table for drawing plans and for holding coffee cups. A separate alcove holds a ceramics kiln. And when the inevitable spills occur, they're easy to clean up because of the smooth-surface tile flooring.

Off to sea while right at home. If you're converting the basement of your house into an added room, you have an opportunity to indulge your taste for a favorite decorative theme. Bright nautical decorations give this room a special flair. In a niche, a prized ship model is framed with netting. Lamps are fashioned from colorful running lights and an anchor. The stairway is edged with fancy ropework, and similar ropework is found elsewhere in the room. Other artifacts, including a steering wheel and a life preserver salvaged from a ship, help carry out the going-to-sea effect. Pay attention to the flooring in this basement. It's asphalt tile, and the designs of signal flags flying from halyards are set right into it. While sometimes overlooked, the floor is usually the largest decorative element in a room; and this means you can plan around it in establishing a theme like this one.

Gourmet dining in the basement! Entertaining can be more fun and less work in an attractive basement room. Use your imagination in decorating, and your room can be as beautiful as this one. Inspired by a collection of menus from famous restaurants, it says, "Bon appétit" the moment guests come down the stairs. Cushioned metal chairs and stools, candelabra, and fringes all over the place set the pace for the decorative theme. A striped awning over the counter hides the lighting and enhances the look of a Parisian bistro. Pierced tinware lanterns add soft illumination at the edges of the room. A multicolored floor shows how well the various patterns of tile go together. As for the menus, they're mounted on metalwork screens that divide the room without wholly obscuring vision. Somebody please pass the hors d'oeuvres.

Could you imagine this as a do-it-yourself project?
Sometimes a young couple buys a house with an "expansion attic," figuring they'll need the extra space when babies arrive. But then the years pass and the children grow older, and there still doesn't seem to be enough money to have the attic finished. Families in such a predicament can take heart when they look at this room, for most of what they see here could be done with their own hands. Installing louvered doors for good cross ventilation. Building storage drawers into the partition between bedroom and bath. (That idea proved itself a wonderful space saver.) Using bows of starchy striped fabric on the corners of the canopy bed, then repeating those elsewhere in the room. A floor like this can be a do-it-yourself job, too. It's linoleum tile, with contrasting feature strips.

A one-room apartment in an attic. Whether you rent it, keep it for guests, or use it to make a mother-in-law happy, a one-room apartment is almost always a good investment. This house had an area in the attic, 18 by 21 feet, that was just waiting for such a use. The apartment was planned with a "living end" and a "working end." In the former the problem of ventilation, common to most attic apartments, was solved by making partitions only rafter-high. Four unpainted chests were remodeled into a dresser-cupboard combination; above them, an old tin pie-chest with lights mounted inside makes a memorable lamp. For a canopy over the bed, a pleated valance was attached directly to the rafters. In the "working end" (see inset), the kitchen window was kept as a source of light by using a work counter as a half partition. The other kitchen wall, which helps form the entrance hall, is a linen and utility closet.

A bright extra bedroom, and not that expensive. If you have access to wasted attic space, maybe it's time to think about how it could become an additional bedroom in your home. If you're at all handy with tools, you probably can do most of the work yourself. And that will save money fast. This room is furnished with a fiberboard material that serves as both interior finish and insulation. It's made in big boards like those on the walls and in a tile form that's installed on the ceiling. Both were nailed in place over a simple wood frame. When you're finished you don't need to paint the fiberboard, because its surface is applied at the factory. With that work done and with a new floor (linoleum, in this case), it's time to enjoy decorating your new room. The quilt is the key here. Its pattern is picked up at the window, in the chair upholstery, and in the footstool. A full-length mirror on the closet door is a convenience, and it also helps to make the room look larger.

The quick-to-build room. In just a few days, an accomplished do-it-yourselfer can turn an attic into an extra room like this. The walls and ceiling are the explanation. They're formed of an inexpensive fiberboard material that decorates and also provides insulation value. The wall panels and ceiling tiles are nailed onto wooden boards used to frame out the attic area. You don't have to bother about painting the fiberboard, because it comes with two coats of paint applied at the factory. Here a comfortable couch doubles as a bed. Nearby is a dressing table with mirror. And on the other side of the room is a desk for homework assignments. Window curtains are of a fabric heavy enough to shut out unwanted light when it's time to turn in for the night.

The "what-do-you-call-it?" room. The people who own this home knew one thing: they needed more room. They needed space for hobbies, for entertaining, for dozens of other activities of a growing family. But it would take a palace—wouldn't it?—to provide for all that. They found their palace in an unused section of their basement. And they saved money by doing much of the work themselves, from installing an asphalt tile floor to putting up insulation board material on the walls and ceiling. They put in storage cabinets, with a magazine rack above them. One portion of the area is closed off tight to form a photography lab. A built-in screen pulls down when guests come in to view movies. Members of the family still don't know what to call their new room, because it has so many functions. Doesn't matter, really. The important thing is that they all enjoy using it.

A young idea for an old attic. Ever notice how, as the family grows, the room in the home seems to contract? The time comes when you have to think about moving to a larger house—or finding more room within your existing home. The latter idea may be entirely practicable for the family with unused attic space. This added bedroom, with a new bath right next door, shows how beautifully the concept can be carried out. Walls and ceiling are covered with a fiberboard material that can be installed by a home handyman or -woman. The "paper cutout" design on the bedspread repeats itself in the treatment of the window valance. A chalkboard mounted on the wall encourages young artists to exercise their talents. As the child grows older, furnishings and decorative elements of the room can be changed to reflect his or her tastes.

One attic finished, two boys happy. With a new baby in the family, and with its two brothers old enough to be rambunctious at times—maybe this is when we need to add a bedroom, the parents agreed. The unfinished attic was the place; they agreed on that, too. Then an idea occurred to them. Nobody remembers who thought of it first, but it went something like this: If we could make it a real boys' room, if we could decorate it in some special way. . . . Look at the result. It's a bunkhouse bedroom for the two boys. They even have their own place to wash up,

in a bathroom behind swinging doors, and that gives the parents some elbow room in their own bath. The bunks are "stagecoach beds," mounted on wheels. That was planned for appearance, but it has a practical side, too. When there's cleaning to be done, they can be rolled to the other side of the room so it's possible to dust without stooping. It was not difficult to find decorating accessories to carry through the Far West theme. And it's not difficult to keep the room spotless, either, thanks to its embossed linoleum flooring.

Opposite:

Once it was a porch. If you're in need of extra space in your home and you have an open porch, don't overlook the advantages that can be gained by using the porch as the basic framework for your new room. For one thing, you'll find that it cuts building costs considerably. For another, the usefulness of an open porch is limited to a few summer months; but converting it to a room gives it year-round utility. Next to the living room and with easy access to the yard, it can quickly become one of the favorite rooms in the

house. This particular porch conversion was planned for use by the whole family. It serves nicely as a retreat for someone who wants seclusion, and it's practical enough to withstand the wear and tear of teen-age youngsters. Furnishings have been kept on the informal side. The high-color accents, used against the colorful simplicity found in the linoleum tile floor, eliminate the need for a lot of decorative accessories. Large windows still give an expansive vista of the out-of-doors.

Opposite top:

Count the opportunities for enjoyment. A basement playroom is one of the best investments you can make in your home. It's a place where members of the family and their friends can enjoy themselves without restraint. At the same time, it saves wear and tear on the rest of the house. Everyone in the family can take part in planning such a room, to assure that each person's own favorite pastime is provided for. This room has a nice high ceiling, so there's room for table tennis. The table at left is set up for games but also is suitable for jigsaw puzzles and serving snacks. A cabinet holding television set and record player serves as a low room divider. Murals showing the outdoors are flanked by curtains suggesting windows. On the far wall, items representing some of the family's special interests are mounted to become usable decorative accessories.

Up on the roof-top, down in the basement? Well, yes, it's possible. When you plan a basement room, you'll find it's the one place in the home where you can give free rein to your imagination. You can even create a roof-top atmosphere like this by painting a "skyscraper" scene on the walls. A bar that's designed to look like a chimney and indirect lighting hidden behind an imitation roof-top wall will help to complete the illusion. So will an awning that juts out from one wall. The wrong floor over basement concrete can cause trouble. The concrete draws up moisture from the ground. As the moisture rises, it becomes alkaline. Some floors can be ruined by alkaline moisture' but not this one. It's asphalt tile, specially made to withstand this damaging condition. Here it's installed with stripes of contrasting colors. Say, is that the sound of traffic down in the street below?

A side porch comes inside. The people who own this home, like so many others, needed extra space. Space for entertaining, for television viewing, for sewing, and for the many other activities of a growing family. They decided they could get that space most economically by enclosing the old side porch. While they were at it, they did something interesting with one of the walls. They framed it out, covered it with a fiberboard interior finish, and turned it into a real conversation piece. It's clearly the focal point of the room. The wall includes a niche to set off a treasured family heirloom of a clock. It is loaded with drawers and storage cabinets and even has a pull-out shelf for serving snacks. A window wall, with draw curtains covering the lower half, provides for privacy while at the same time admitting plenty of light from outside.

Beauty treatment for an old cellar. This room was created in the cellar of a Lancaster, Pennsylvania house that was sixty-five years old! If you had visited it before (inset 1), you might have thought it would never be good for anything but storing shutters. Just look at it now. It's a room you'd be proud to entertain guests in. Those spacious brick seats, less costly than furniture, are good looking and comfortable. Cushions are inexpensive, bunk-size cotton mattresses, covered with awning fabric. The handy "magazine tree" in the center of the room is simple to build, and it hides an ugly supporting column. In the music corner (inset 2), a counter with storage cupboards below extends along one wall for serving snacks. Two coach lights are mounted on short posts to give the room an appropriate long-time-ago feeling. Retained were the beams overhead, and a fiberboard tile ceiling has been installed between them.

1

2

Finding room for a puppet theater. Unused attic space can often be tranformed into an extra room in the house, easily and economically. The family in this home has varied interests. The adults like to knit and to paint—and, sometimes, just to relax with one another. They wanted a room that would accommodate those activities. But they're thoughtful parents, and they wanted to make sure the children were not forgotten. The area they developed has room for everybody's interests. The puppet theater even has space for an audience, if it isn't too large an audience! Lighting fixtures are recessed into the ceiling, with lamps to provide more intense illumination for close work. The resilient flooring underfoot, the fiberboard panels on the walls, and the ceiling tiles all were chosen for practicality as well as economy.

Basement for a lady with a green thumb. If gardening's your passion, here's how basement space can be utilized as a gardener's workshop as well as a laundry. Bulbs and tools as well as socks and shirts can be rinsed conveniently at the wash tubs that separate the gardener's corner from the laundry. Placed out into the room instead of against a wall, the tubs can be used from either side. The laundry portion of the room includes a complete sewing center. Sewing machine, work space, and mending equipment are right at hand for quick repairs. For the lady with a green thumb, open bins with hinged glass doors keep flower seeds, bulbs, and catalogs in sight, yet they're neatly separated. Row upon row of extra-deep drawers store the small tools and equipment that clutter most gardeners' benches, and there's a cabinet desk with plentiful storage space.

A reason to enjoy staying at home. Almost any couple likes to go out for an evening's entertainment, at least occasionally. Nothing wrong with that. But with a basement fitted up like this, it's also possible to invite friends in for a supper-club atmosphere right at home. If balloons are festive, this interior scheme makes you think of party time. The balloon motif is captured in lighting fixtures, in the bases of round tables and stools, in the curtain fabric, even in the polka dots on the drinking glasses. The curtains can be drawn back to reveal the music corner on the far wall. The asphalt tile flooring is installed in a smart gray and white layout that plays up the room's overall color scheme. And this floor is smooth enough for dancing. Talk about spending a night out without ever leaving home!

Two families live under one roof—happily. Here's an attic apartment that's specially designed to make it easy to live with parents or married children in your home. For one thing, it's self-contained, with a modern kitchenette and bathroom tucked away behind the partitions. For another, it offers extra features that say more eloquently than words that the people who live here are honored guests. The fireplace adds to the homelike atmosphere, as does the skylight cut into the ceiling. The bright, cheerful color scheme and the luxurious comfort of the furnishings make the room as inviting as a downstairs living room. The flooring was chosen with care. It's cork tile, with a natural color and texture that add a glowing warmth to almost any interior. The table serves double duty. Placed next to the kitchenette for convenient serving, it can be pushed through a wall slot to provide extra counter space while you're preparing meals.

Pushing the living room out onto the porch. Much of this room—the portion with a sloped ceiling—was once an open porch. It adjoined a living room that the family felt was cramped and inadequate. So they decided to expand the room by taking advantage of the structural framework that already was in place on the porch. Walls containing French doors were removed, opening the space and giving it a fresh new appearance. Now there was room for a piano, for television viewing, and for comfortable lounge furniture. A wall of full-length windows was added. Together with corners full of potted plants and a handsome bird cage, this helps to retain the outdoorsy feel of the old porch. The flooring is linoleum in several patterns, including directional feature strips.

The master bedroom moves to the basement. It may seem an unusual idea, but this room demonstrates how practical it can be. Actually, in many an older house like this one, space and opportunity are waiting for a touch of imagination. This area was like a lot of basements, with little to say for it. But it had more possibilities than at first appeared. A few hours of bulldozer time paid off. Grading opened up the rear wall of the basement; and that made space for a patio right outside, with glass doors leading to it. In an adjoining wall, high windows admit still more daylight. Between the twin beds is a control panel that permits the homeowners to light almost any area in their house or their yard without leaving the master bedroom. The flooring of asphalt tile withstands the potentially damaging effect of alkaline moisture found in basement subfloors.

An unfinished second floor turns into extra living space. Simplified, informal decoration makes it more practical and less costly today to turn the unfinished second floor of a home into attractive space that the whole family can use. Here's a family room that doubles as a music room. But that isn't all. Plastic curtains pull out from the television divider wall to shut off two bedrooms—one with double bunks, the other with a dressier canopy bed. A bathroom at right serves the entire area. Windows have been cut into the end walls of the house so streams of sunlight can flood into both bedrooms. The flooring is of an almost seamless vinyl sheet material, with a design that suggests homespun fabric. Though the surface is smooth and easy to swish clean with a sponge mop, it looks as though it's rough-textured; and that fits nicely with the brick and wood effects found elsewhere in the room.

A "sunken garden" living room in the basement.
Opening up an old basement made this attractive living room possible. A few hours of grading around the rear of the house changed the contours of the back yard. Now you step up to a small patio just outside, then step up again to a new level, with comfortable wicker garden chairs. The living room itself is dominated by a large, low table, whose mar-resistant top is fine for serving snacks.

The natural look of brick and open wooden beams, coupled with an abundance of potted flowers, helps to remind us that the room's decorative theme was inspired by the out-of-doors. Serving as the base for the color scheme is a floor of vinyl-content tile. Smooth, colorful and easy to clean, this type of flooring is suitable for do-it-yourself installation because it can be shaped to fit unusual corners with an ordinary pair of scissors.

A village green that's inviting in any weather. Let it rain! Let it snow! The picnic party is still on. For this bright village green is indoors. It's a basement that's been turned into a party room. Fancy and expensive? No, not really. Most of the furniture has had experience elsewhere, but that makes it more authentic and more enjoyable to use. The table and chairs, for example, came from a local café. The park benches were bought at an antique store. The bandstand is simply constructed, with scroll-work cut from plywood. It's a place to show off the family's musical talents, and it houses a record player, too. The trash receptable, with its swinging lid, is a whimsical touch that helps carry out the "public park" theme. Behind the snack counter is a laundry, though you'd never know that when a party is in progress.

"Sundae" basement solves everyday problems. This room belongs to some of the luckiest teen-agers, and cleverest parents, in the world. As recently as a month ago, upstairs, it was anybody's guess who owned the living room—the high-school set or the grownups. Now everybody's happy, especially Mother. For not even dancing feet and spilled drinks will damage this basement room. One reason is its floor of vinyl-content tile. Spilled popcorn sweeps up quickly, because the plastic surface is so smooth. The flooring is laid tile by tile, so it's easy for even a do-it-yourselfer to put together special designs like the one in this room. Mounted behind the counter are simple recipes for whipping up various kinds of soda-fountain treats. The fireplace wall is painted a light color to help brighten the room, and the stairs are finished in a striped effect that echoes the stripes of the couch upholstery.

Can a basement this rich-looking be economical?
Here's the kind of room that leads guests to say, "Now why didn't I think of doing that with my basement?" Actually, it was quite a simple matter to turn an old, empty basement into a room that offers space for parties or family fun, with almost no morning-after clean-up trouble. One of the main explanations for its economy is its floor of asphalt tile. See that custom inset? It's designed to complement the upholstery fabric, which gives the room its primary decorative theme. Accessible from both sides, the fireplace includes a handy butcher's-block shelf for preparing foods and a rack from which to hang pans and cooking utensils. Soft lighting gleams through pierced-tin lanterns, hung from the open-beam ceiling. An inexpensive crossbar treatment, reminiscent of the floor inset, dresses the high basement windows.

The car made way for the family. When a family grows too big for the house, it's a case of either moving to a larger one or finding more space in the existing house. Often it's possible to choose the latter course if you look around with an open mind. An attached garage can sometimes provide a splendid solution to the space problem. An economical one, too, because roof, walls, and foundation are ready and waiting. Once the dividing wall was broken through, creating this handsome family room adjacent to the home's kitchen was largely a do-it-yourself affair. The vinyl-content flooring was designed especially for installation by a home handyman or woman, using just a brush and a pair of scissors for tools. It was such a success that it was put down in the kitchen, too, in a harmonizing color. There are young children in this home; that's why a pull-together screen was included to separate the kitchen from the family room. When it's not needed, it slides away just behind the kitchen cupboard.

An attic room with two boys' names on it. The brothers were growing older, and they felt it was time they had a room that they could fix up to suit their own interests. Their parents agreed, inasmuch as they had other ideas for the room downstairs that the boys had been sharing. Besides, they knew there was unused attic space in the house. At a series of family meetings, the ideas came pouring forth. Everybody had a say. And when it was time to go to work on that attic, even the boys pitched in. They helped Dad install the flooring. It's a linoleum tile. But, whereas most floor tile is square, this particular type came in a 6-inch by 12-inch shape, in a styling that resembled parquetry. When the project was finished, everybody agreed that the new floor was a fine complement to the natural wood-grain finishes elsewhere in the room. And can't you just see how much the brothers enjoyed putting in their own special decorative touches?

A place for treasured antiques. Turning a basement into a recreation room is an easy way to get extra living space. In this home it also provided a place for displaying the results of years of antique collecting, and the room decoration contributes to the effect. The old wood-burning stove works; it's vented into the chimney next to it. Above the vaulted hearth is a shelf for early lighting devices, other items made of wrought iron, and a turn-of-the-century decoy. At left the lighted shelves hold redware and painted tinware. In front of the bench is a hand loom for miniature needlework. The bench is an antique, but the chairs are of recent construction. They're cut-down barrels, with padding and upholstery added. The lamp is made from a portion of a drumhead capstan. The flooring? Definitely modern. It's a vinyl-content tile, with offset yellow feature strips to add visual interest.

The Spouter Tavern drops into the basement. If you're converting an unused basement area into an added room for your home, you may as well turn your imagination loose and develop the room around a special interest your family has. In this family, the interest was nautical. Look how a few accessories have perfected that theme. At center stage is the replica of a ship's figurehead. Beside the stairway are an old anchor and an authentic ship's chronometer. The spouting whale above the ship model is cut out of copper sheeting. A fireplace and simple but comfortable furniture complete the ensemble. An open-beam ceiling lends the look of an old New England inn. And the eye-catching "compass rose" design in the floor? That can be installed, like the rest of the vinyl-content flooring, by any do-it-yourselfer who's handy around the house.

A crow's-nest for solitude. The owners of this home needed extra space, and they thought the attic might be just the place to find it. What they had in mind was a place of solitude, a place for quiet reading and knitting. By the time they finished planning it, everybody in the family had contributed ideas for special features. The reading and knitting are provided for, all right, but there's so much more in this room. It can even be used for overnight guests now. The extensions on the day beds, with drawers included, are supported by "trees" that have artificial leaves and also serve as support for the hanging lamps. There's a table for games and snacks and a pull-down screen for showing color slides. A large window brings in sunlight from outside. Solitude? Well, that hasn't worked out so well. Problem is, everybody in the family likes to use this room, and it's seldom a quiet place now.

Need more space? Consider enclosing a porch. This family had an open porch that stretched all the way across the back of the house. What it needed more than that, though, was extra space inside. Put those two facts together, and the solution was basic: enclose the porch, and we'll have the new family room we want. That's just the way it worked out. Fortunately, the porch was just off the kitchen. So the family room and the step-up kitchen can share counter space, with stools turning the counter into a lunch bar from the family room side. With small chairs beside it, the low coffee table doubles as a children's work table. There's space for television watching, of course, and also sewing. Alongside the Dutch door, which admits daylight but provides security for the youngsters, is a home-made screen that adds a decorative touch. The flooring is a smooth, almost seamless vinyl sheet material that's easy to keep clean.

The attic becomes a family hideaway. Singly or as a group, members of the family tend to move toward this room as if it were a magnet. It isn't difficult to figure out why. The family needed more room, and they turned to unused attic space to solve their problem. Solve it they did, for this new room accommodates everybody's interests. It's a quiet area for homework or for catching up with correspondence. It's a television viewing room or a place for concentration on needlework. It's a party room or a place where the teen-agers can entertain their friends after school. The raised hearth vents into the house's existing chimney. Open beams in the ceiling are carried vertically down the walls. That provides unity to the decorating scheme. So does the vinyl sheet flooring, which has a custom design set into it for accent.

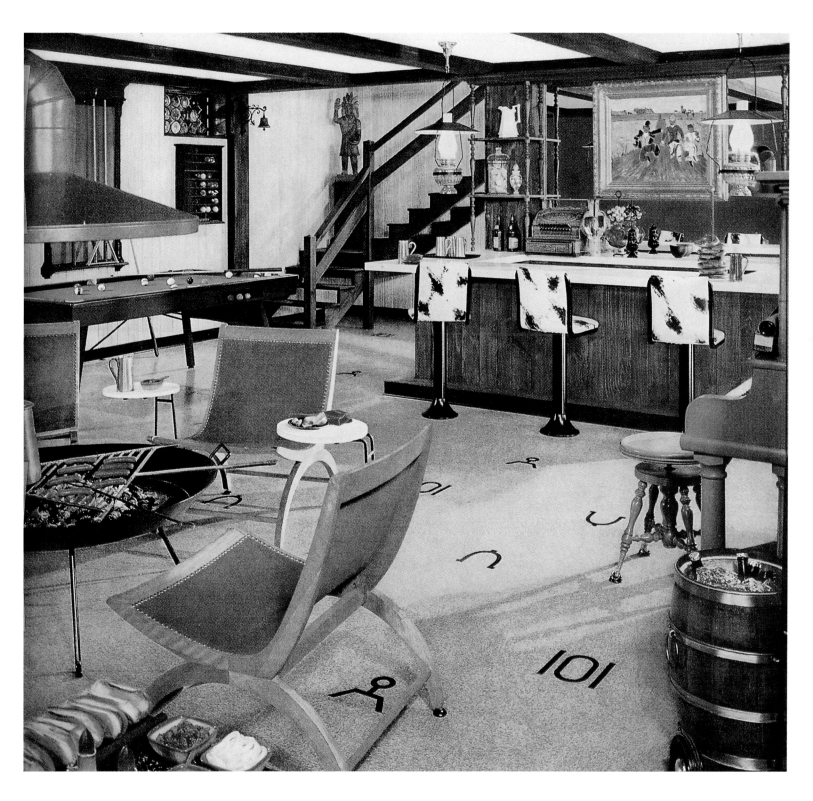

This way down to Old Wyoming. Imagine youself as the hostess, greeting guests as they arrive: "We're having the party in the basement. Come on down!" Catch the look on their faces as, for the first time, they see how you've turned that extra space into a theme room that anybody would find delightful to entertain in. The cash register on the counter is just like one you'd see in a western movie. The stools are covered with artificial calfskin. Other furnishings, such as the barrel filled with iced drinks and the vented barbecue grille, add their own special decorative flavor. The flooring, now that's what sets the style for the whole room. It's a vinyl-content tile that can be installed by a do-it-yourselfer. And yes, a do-it-yourselfer can also put in the cattle-brand insets that are so distinctive. Please don't shoot the piano player.

Chapter 8

Hallways, apartments, and offices

In its advertisements of the 1950s, Armstrong wanted to demonstrate that its products were suitable for every room in the house. Along with its concentration on the main rooms, the company devoted attention to other types of rooms, less frequently thought of, such as hallways, entryways, and in-home apartments and offices. These rooms, like all the others, offer inspiring glimpses into what can be done with imagination, even on a limited budget.

A one-room apartment with a Brittany bed. The woman who owns this home had planned to renovate a spare bedroom, then rent it as a furnished room. But a suggestion from a friend who was an interior designer changed her mind. "No, not a furnished room," said the friend. "We will make it a little apartment. Then you will get three times as much rent." While she was looking over the room, she suddenly stopped, peering into a corner. "There we will put a Brittany bed," she exclaimed, "like the one that is in my old home in France." That proved to be a wonderful idea for a one-room apartment. With the curtains closed, the bed can be left made up all the time. More than that, the bed sets the decorative theme for the entire room. Now it's complete, decorated in French Provincial style. An imported wood stove, purchased at an antiques store, offers warmth. A parquet-effect floor of linoleum provides a quiet, distinguished foil for the other furnishings.

Making room for a parent. When a parent reaches an age at which it's no longer sensible to continue living alone, one of his or her adult children can sometimes find space to create an apartment. In this instance, Mother was able to sell her old house, then move into these new quarters at her daughter's home. They once were the garage. A bay window has been put in where the garage door used to be; and built-ins, such as a desk and book shelves, have been added. The garage was next to the kitchen, so it didn't cost much to bring in plumbing for a bathroom. Now the apartment has a sleeping-dressing alcove (see inset) that is set off from the living area by louvered doors and by a smart triangle design in the floor of asphalt tile. Special effects like this are possible at no extra cost because the floor tiles are laid individually.

An office that retains the comforts of home. Years before home offices became widely accepted, people in business recognized that attractive surroundings can help reduce the tension of hectic days. Work hours in an office like this are more enjoyable, more productive. With its magazine rack and its comfortable seating, the room is well-suited for visitors, too, including clients and customers. Potted plants contribute a homey feel. Floor and walls are covered with cork tile. Its natural texture and nutlike tones reflect good taste and prestige, and it provides a warm but neutral framework for the stronger colors used in the room's decoration. "Fins" that extend from the wall facing the desk offer visual interest and set off the sculpted wall hanging.

Opposite:

A library that serves as a guest room, too. What do you do when you have only one extra room in your home but you want to use it in two ways? Unstopper your idea bottle, and see what your imagination can come up with. In this home, the husband had wanted a library. His wife said, "Yes, but. . . ." She had been hoping that the spare room could be used for guests. Here's how both had their dreams come true. The secret lay in the roll-away beds. The husband designed special bookcases to hide the folded-up beds during the day. At night, the front panels are reversed and become headboards for the beds (see inset). When the shirred curtains are dropped and the reversible rug is turned, the library shifts into a guest room for two. An upright mirror transforms the library desk into a dressing table. And some of the guests like it so much they don't want to leave!

Which came first, laundry or playroom? Doesn't matter, really, because this basement room serves as both. It's a way to get the most use out of a utility space like this: make it serve as a comfortable place to do the laundry, and as an inviting room for parties as well. The transformation from one room to another takes place with the help of folding doors and a clever work table that turns into a beverage bar. In a few minutes the laundry equipment can be completely concealed, and you're ready for guests (see inset). The floor design is only one of the countless effects that can be created with tiles. Because the tiles are installed one by one, it's simple to make up a special layout to reflect your own preferences or to carry out the design theme of the room. A blackboard on the wall helps the family keep up with its busy schedule.

From old back parlor to inviting entrance hall. Reconditioning an older home, top to bottom, can be challenging but enjoyable—especially if you're not constrained by preconditioned thinking. In this formerly out-of-date residence, the entrance hall is now one of the most striking rooms in the house. It once was the back parlor (see inset). The transition began when a window was changed into a door, and space was partitioned off for a powder room. Cutting the big floral-leaf wallpaper to frame wall mirrors is an idea that can have many applications. So is the trick of using old porch posts to support a handsome home-made table. Bringing an old Victorian chest back to life with refurbishing is another money-saving suggestion that can be used in almost any room that's being redecorated. Spatter linoleum adds a dash of excitement to the new entranceway.

An added room provides an apartment for Mother. In this one-room apartment built onto her married daughter's home, Mother has every comfort and convenience. She even has her own outside entrance. Whether spending a quiet hour in needlework or entertaining a friend for lunch, she lives in a bright, airy setting that gives her as much privacy as she wants yet keeps her near her caring family. The poster bed is closed off by curtains and valance that match the window treatment. Behind those curtains, the bed can remain made up all day. At nighttime (see inset) a lamp on a step table beside the bed provides light for reading. The linoleum flooring has all the beauty of costly wood parquet. But this flooring has no splinters and no open seams, and it doesn't have to be sanded or varnished. What's more, it has the ability to go with any furnishings.

A small hall that calls, "Welcome, you-all!" One way or another, the entryway of a home says something to visitors. Even a small entrance hall can go a long way toward making your home more gracious and making your guests more welcome. This one looks more spacious than it really is because of the big wall mirror and the specially designed floor of vinyl tile. It gives a cordial welcome in all kinds of weather, too, because tracked-in dirt or water doesn't harm this modern plastic flooring. Footprints wipe away in a trice without leaving a trace! In the adjoining powder room, which has a dressing table so guests can freshen up as they arrive, the flooring tile is installed in a contrasting color. A starry constellation of a chandelier provides plenty of illumination in the hallway without causing a glare.

Inspirational Notes